W. D. Campbell: Naturalist and Teacher

W. D. Campbell:
Naturalist and Teacher

Written and edited by
Mary and Ken Jackson

THE WYCHWOOD PRESS

Our books may be ordered from bookshops or (post free) from
Jon Carpenter Publishing, Alder House, Market Street,
Charlbury OX7 3PH
01608 811969
e-mail: wychwood@joncarpenter.co.uk
Credit card orders should be phoned or faxed to 01689 870437 or
01608 811969
Please ask for our free catalogue

First published in 2003 by
The Wychwood Press
an imprint of Jon Carpenter Publishing
Alder House, Market Street, Charlbury, Oxfordshire OX7 3PH

ISBN 1 902279 01 8

Printed in England by Antony Rowe, Chippenham

CONTENTS

Publisher's note

This book has been a labour of love by Mary and Ken Jackson, working from Bill Campbell's own archive of his Country Diaries as well as other documents, together with tape recordings made by Ken.

We are grateful to Guardian Newspapers Ltd for permission to reproduce many of the 'Country Diaries' that Bill write for the *Guardian*.

We are also indebted to Peter and Phyllis Mond for organising the transcription of the tape of a talk given by Bill in Chadlington, and for borrowing the photograph on page 11 from Cholsey Museum; to Judy and Stuart Dewey for the quotation from *Change at Cholsey Again!* on page 11; and to Hilda Pipe and Jo Dunn for checking the names of birds and plants and their spellings and for editing the finished book.

FOREWORD

Whether home is in the town or the country, the countryside of Britain has a special place in people's hearts. Its rich diversity and the minutiae of daily country living provide for us a fascination and an escape from the stresses and strains of a life made ever more technological and bureaucratic. The keenest observers of the earth we move in don't wallow in nostalgia or embrace sentimental conservationalism, they live and breathe the countryside as it is with its seasonal and political fluctuations, and restore through nature our faith in life. Among the best instinctive observers of the natural life we live will always be diarists. W.D. Campbell – Bill – began writing a Country Diary for the *Guardian* in 1964. His vast knowledge of bird life, natural history and gardening was eagerly devoured by readers.

He did not miss one week – even writing from his hospital bed. For more than 30 years readers had the privilege of sharing Bill's Oxfordshire garden and followed his exploits as one of the longest serving ringers under the national bird-marking scheme. His annual visits to the Isles of Scilly and Portland Bill kept readers up to date on the passage of bird life. But it was the personal nuggets that Bill threaded through his diaries that took him into the readers' hearts and minds and brought enquiries and 'get well' cards when age left him less fit than he would have liked. It was through Bill that many people discovered a love of the countryside.

A perfect illustration of Bill's ability as communicator is illustrated in a tale in the book, *Walk Humble, My Son* by Eric Moss, which tells of the writer's life, growing up in Ascott-under-Wychwood between 1918 and 1939. Eric Moss, who died in 2001, and his brother enjoyed ferreting as boys and they fed the ferrets with small birds caught at night with clap nets (a pair of canes, bent at the top like hockey sticks with a light net fixed to the canes' top half). That was until the day came when 'a bird-loving teacher showed us the error of our ways. Though we still caught the birds we put rings on their legs, logged the time, place, bird, sex and then let them go'. The teacher was, of course, Bill. Eric Moss goes on to describe how he and Bill caught a great grey shrike. 'William was so excited that we went straight to his home where we looked up his books to confirm his catch while the bird sat docilely on my wrist. It appeared to be some kind of hawk. A few days later a rather long record of the bird's capture appeared in the local press, where we read that it was very scarce and that the last known specimen was shot at Banbury in 1880.'

As an editor, I could not have had a more talented, conscientious and professional writer. Our weekly conversations on the phone were a welcome diversion from office life. At the service in November 1994 to celebrate Bill's long and fruitful life, I spoke with a woman who had never met Bill nor had she had much interest in the countryside. But her parents read his diaries and pointed them out to her. She immediately became a loyal fan. 'When I read that he had died,' she said, 'I wanted to say goodbye and thank you to a friend.' He was, indeed, a dear friend. Thank you, Bill.

Jeanette Page, July 2000

'Walk Humble, My Son' – Growing up in Ascott-under-Wychwood, 1918-1939 by Eric R. Moss is published by The Wychwood Press, price £8.

1

THE BEGINNINGS OF
WHAT WAS TO COME

William Donald Campbell was better known by his contemporaries as WD, and by his close friends as just plain Bill, although to his family and a few long-standing friends he was always Donald. But by any name, here was a man in a million.

He was born in 1905 in Dorset of Highland Scottish parents. From a very early age he showed an insatiable curiosity for wildlife and as time went on and his knowledge grew deeper, a great respect and understanding developed for all things natural, both fauna and flora. He never tried to improve upon nature, but, with a keen observer's eye, he watched it closely in its different stages and was ready to be surprised and to learn something new every day of his life. Nor did he keep this accumulated knowledge and joy for the outdoor life to himself, but shared it with all those who showed interest, especially the young.

His early education was in village schools in Co. Down and the Cotswold fringe of Oxfordshire, later gaining a scholarship to the City of Oxford High School. Intending to make teaching his career, he went to Culham Teachers' Training College and his first teaching post was in the East End of London. This was followed by posts as specialist teacher of Gardening, Biology and Natural History in West Oxfordshire. He was a Headmaster in Oxfordshire and Berkshire and wrote for the *Gardeners' Chronicle*, *The Countryman*, *The Guardian* and *The Oxford Mail*.

His first book, *Bird-Watching as a Hobby*, appeared in 1959 followed by *Birds of Town and Village* in 1965. This is a book with magnificent plates by Basil Ede, and a faithful record in both word and picture of fifty-six British birds that may be seen in and around our towns and villages. Bill showed his wonderful way with words and, as in his lectures, broadcasts and other writings on natural history, he often used a small phrase that pin-pointed a bird for us. For instance, when contrasting the carrion crow with the rook, he says 'the carrion crow is an individualistic free-booter rather than a mass-conforming commuter', and he writes of 'the barn owl's disembodied face silently floating towards one', or the little tree creeper's penetrating call, 'reminiscent of hard cloth being cut by fast-working tailor's scissors'.

The family of eight first arrived in Oxfordshire from Ireland in November 1910. They had been living in Northern Ireland at Portaferry on the edge of Strangford Lough. They suffered sea-sickness crossing from Ulster. But, at the beginning of the journey as they passed through the shipyards at Belfast, they saw a wonderful sight, a large imposing and beautiful ship with its lights ablaze in the growing darkness.

'Look, Willie,' Bill recalled his father saying, 'that is the *Titanic*. They say she is unsinkable. You will be able to tell folk that you have seen her. Behind her, where there is a great flare of lights and clanging of iron, the *Olympic* is being completed.'

His father was to be Head Gardener at the Cornbury estate near Charlbury in Oxfordshire, then owned by the Watney family. It was dark as they drove up the drive in a horse-drawn wagon from Charlbury station, with literally one-candle-power lamps fixed to the wagon to light their way. As they approached the cottage in a corner of Cornbury Park adjoining the forest, where they were to live for the next twenty-one years, the horse slowed down to negotiate a sharp downhill bend and five-year-old Bill saw pairs of gleaming points of light in the sky, sometimes red, sometimes green, and then closer, all round them they winked, coming and going in the dark – and he was frightened. His father assured him, 'They are only a herd of fallow deer in the park! It's the reflection of our lights in the deer's eyes. You see, our wagon lights are being reflected from the deer's eyes. Deer have lived in the forest for 600 years, at least. They are curious and wonder what we are and if we are likely to attack them, and are really far more frightened than you. Tomorrow, we'll try to see them in daylight. They are beautiful, shy, wild beasts, you'll find out.' So it was as Bill said, 'I never forgot this eerie reception party. I got terrific lights at one end of the journey and these mystery lights at the other end.'

His interest in natural history had really begun and so he spent his formative years in idyllic surroundings – the four-acre gardens of this stately home in West Oxfordshire, surrounded by the ancient forest of Wychwood, where he lived from the age of five until 1931. Many were the walks he took in Wychwood Forest with his father. He wrote:

> My father, a Head Gardener of the old Scottish school, was just as interested in the wild flora of the area as he was in the more exotic orchids, grapes, bananas, peaches and paw-paws in the vast range of glass-houses. And having acquired a fair smattering of Latin from a sound Scottish education, he imprinted me at an early age with the knowledge that plants had both common and scientific names – I can still recall an early incident during a walk in the forest. 'Now look, Willie,' Dad pointed out in pedantic Victorian fashion, 'This is *atropa belladonna* – in the vulgar tongue, deadly nightshade, and if you ate three or four of these black berries, they would kill you!'

Bill was the only member of the family not to be born in Scotland, which used to annoy him since his parents, and his ancestors going back to 1601, were Highland and he considered he was pure bred Highland Scots. Until one day, when he was older and reading Thomas Hardy instead of Scott and Burns and so on, he said to his Gaelic-speaking mother, 'Mum, I lived in the same village as Thomas Hardy, I wonder if I ever saw him?' And she replied, 'Och indeed, Tom Hardy often looked in your pram and said what a bonny babe you were.' Ever since this knowledge came to him, Bill used to say with a twinkle, he was reconciled to having been born in England. Bill was to read and re-read all Thomas Hardy wrote and often quoted from his poems.

If Bill was a bonny babe, he grew up to be a handsome man, with no airs and graces, who seemed to dress to suit the countryside, unpretentiously in tweedy muted shades that always looked comfortable and well-worn, and he was rarely without his pipe, which added to his homely and thoughtful appearance. Although Bill was essentially a private professional man, he was on the other hand easy to talk to and very good company when the occasion demanded. Deeply knowledgeable of both natural history and human nature, he had a merry sense of humour and those lucky enough to attend his lectures were always in for a treat. In due course, he was President of the Oxford Ornithological Society and chairman of the first committee set up by the British Trust for Ornithology to investigate the effects of toxic chemicals on wildlife. He was then on the Joint Committee of that body and the Royal Society for the Protection of Birds. Although his early interests were mainly floral, thanks to a form-master at his Oxford school, by a spell of butterfly collecting, he unconsciously became familiar with some of the more interesting birds in the garden: the redstart which nested in a disused pipe in their cottage wall, the pied wagtails which regularly found their way into a greenhouse to nest beneath a tub of *Lapageria*, the swallows frequenting stables and sheds, and even nesting on a noisy telephone bell in the porch, the barn owl with young on top of a pile of hampers in the fruit-room, and spotted flycatchers affixing their nests between the trained fruit-trees and the walls. But the turning-point in his interest occurred some time in 1923 as he has related,

'I have not the precise date, except for just "Easter". Then, 'one of the men' [a term which distinguished the garden labourers from 'the bothy-men', the budding professionals who lived on the premises and wore blue serge aprons] brought a bird which had become entangled in some netting, to my father. He, familiar with snipe in his boyhood haunts in Caithness and Sutherland, recognised it as one of this family, but, and I still do not know why, sensed that it was not an 'ordinary' specimen, and therefore suggested that I should show it to his employer, Vernon Watney.

'What have you got there, my boy?'

'It's a sort of snipe. Dad thought you'd like to see, sir.'

'Bring it inside.'

After the squire's reference to many books in his extensive library, he said, 'Will you count his tail feathers?' – which I duly did.

'Sixteen, sir.'

'Good gracious, it's a great snipe! The common snipe has only fourteen. Let me see. That's the first record since 1878 for Oxfordshire. Now, what do you propose to do with it?'

'I shall let it go, sir'.

'Well done, my boy.' He patted me on the shoulder and went with me to the terrace and we let this great Snipe go. Now this was the good old slow-going days of penny post. At eight o'clock next morning, there was a knock at the door and there was the postman with a parcel. It had been less than twenty-four hours since the great snipe had been released, when I was rewarded by the receipt of two books from Foyle's of London, Johns' *British Birds in their Haunts* and Aplin's *Birds of Oxfordshire*. From that day of the great snipe, my interest in birds really began.

2

SCHOOL DAYS – BOY AND MASTER

B ill attended Charlbury School as a young boy and in March 1917 he sat the Junior County Scholarship. On April 19th he was awarded a scholarship to Oxford High School and his school was granted a half day holiday. He returned to Charlbury in January 1925 as Pupil Teacher, where he remained until July of that year, when he began his teacher training at Culham Teacher Training College, followed by a teacher's post in London. In September 1928, however, he returned to Charlbury School, specialising in science and gardening, using an area of ground which was to take up two acres of the Spendlove Close. It became such a success under his guidance, that an article appeared in a newspaper:

> It is very doubtful if the Charlbury school gardens have their equal in the County. Roughly speaking, they are about a couple of acres in extent, beautifully laid out, with well-kept flower beds and vegetable plots. A portion of the field was taken over some eighteen months ago, and the remainder last October, and the development which has taken place in so short a time is distinctly creditable to Mr. Campbell, who is the horticultural director, and to the boys and girls themselves.
>
> Everything on the plot is the work of the scholars, from the large and well constructed tool-house to the bee-hives, the tenants of which form an additional opportunity to study. The abundance of space available has made possible the introduction of poultry, which not only gives the opportunity to practical instruction in this useful department, but provides eggs for the cookery department and also assists the 'restaurant' for the midday meal.

In the year 2000 events concerning the site of the Spendlove School, which was built after Bill's time as a Charlbury schoolmaster, led Diana Potten to talk to an older resident for the local publication, *The Charlbury Chronicle*, about those days when the Spendlove was not covered in tarmac for car parking, when there were no recycling bins and certainly no 'bomb site' in the corner of the grounds:

The Spendlove used to be a beautiful spot in Charlbury. It was the site of the gardens belonging to the old school on the Playing Close and there were six painted seats there. During the day young mothers used to come with their prams and sit there enjoying the flowers. In the evenings the older people would gather there and sit around chatting. The gardens were a picture. It was a big area and it was split by the right of way from Nine Acres lane, which came out just above the fountain. The paths were grass and there were large flower beds that changed with the seasons. Rambler roses grew on rustic pole work. In the four corners were the vegetable gardens used to supply the school kitchen with fresh vegetables.

The garden was cultivated by the boys from the school. When they reached the age of eleven and went into the senior school, they had to spend one afternoon a week in the garden. Usually two boys were allocated a plot in the vegetable garden and from this learnt all about growing vegetables. They would also learn about the sowing of flowers in the spring and the pruning of roses. There was a large shed on the Nine Acres side of the garden, with tools to suit all sizes of boy. It was a great honour to be given the key of this shed and to be asked to dig up the vegetables for the school dinner. It was also a thrill to be allowed to use the big motor mower – cast iron with a huge grass box. If the weather was bad there were lectures on growing plants. They had to make plans of a plot and think about crop rotation. The boys did not leave school without knowing quite a lot about gardening and they developed some very good muscles!

When Bill Campbell was a young teacher at the school he was the master in charge of the garden. He made it fun and very interesting. One day a boy had his first go with the mower. He was on Cloud Nine and oblivious to anything else. Bill suggested that as he was cutting, we should walk behind him and put stones in his pocket and see how long it was before he noticed. He was so preoccupied with his job that he never did realise what we were up to!

Bill sometimes had a bird cage trap in the garden. When he trapped a bird, he removed it very carefully and taught the boys all about it. When he had finished, he would ring the bird with a number and then release it.

The interesting thing is that there was never any vandalism in the gardens. Nobody pinched any vegetables or dropped any litter. The only thing that did happen once, was that a boy found some blue paint and decided to paint some of the tulips blue. The headmaster soon found out who was to blame, and when the boy was asked why he had done it, he said he thought it would be a good idea to have some blue tulips for a change!

It was said that the gardens were the best in the county. Certainly it was a really beautiful place in Charlbury. Maybe if the building on Spendlove does not eventuate, the site might once more become a peaceful and attractive garden.

Martin Kirk recalls:

One day when Bill was teaching gardening a boy found a coin, it was recognised as a small coin from the reign of Henry VIII.

'Do you know who that is?' Bill asked, indicating the sovereign's head.

'Aye sir, I does.'

'Who is it then?'

'That's easy,' replied the boy, 'that be Charles Laughton!'

Bill was driven by a pride in a job well done and was not slow in his praise, which must have been an inspiration to his pupils. He kept his eye on progress in the horticultural scene by visiting the Chelsea Flower Show at least in 1934, 1935, 1937 and 1939, and was granted leave of absence to go there by the Director of Education. He took the school children to Agricultural Shows and other schools were brought to visit the Charlbury School gardens, for they had become a show-piece of distinction. In one of the school's inspection reports, it was stated, 'The elements of Biology are carefully and systematically taught by an enthusiast for natural history, but the boys seem to be more impressed by his lessons than the girls. As indicative of the spirit aroused, it may be mentioned that a more or less casual call on the children for the specimens of vipers etc. to be found in the neighbourhood, resulted on the day of inspection in a goodly collection, and old boys are said to join in such naturalist investigations, as they do also in the observation of local bird life, which is systematically studied out of school hours under the master's inspiration and expert guidance. Scientific value attaches to the results of the investigations, such as the recent one into the contents of the pellets of the little owl, the result of which counters the official verdict that the bird is harmful. It is also a great thing that an interest is being created in pupils which may perhaps prove life-long.'

May Alderton was on the teaching staff with Bill and on July 29th 1937, the school log entry reads, 'A presentation was made to Mr Campbell and Miss Alderton on behalf of the staff and scholars of Charlbury School on the occasion of their forthcoming marriage.' And so began a long and happy life together, which was sadly to be marred by a great tragedy much later on in their lives.

Bob Dempster was a pupil at the school in about 1934 when Bill and May were teaching there. He recalls,

> The sessions with him were quite memorable: amongst other lessons, he took us working in the old school gardens, and on nature walks in Wigwell, where he would try to get us to identify different bird calls, some task with a large class of children, many of whom had different ideas, even this did not deter him.
>
> His knowledge of birds was immense and he would state that if ever we could take him a bird that he could not identify, he would give anyone half a crown, a princely sum in those days. However, my father used to breed and show Yorkshire canaries, he also had some cross breed finches. Without letting me in on the plot, he asked me one morning to take a dead bird to Bill Campbell and tell him that he had found it under the apple tree in Lee Place Park, could he tell us what it was? Later that evening Mr Campbell came to the house saying he had been unable to name it, and on offering his half crown, he was told the true facts – the bird was a cross breed. No money changed hands. That, I believe, was the nearest he came to losing his money! Charlbury of the thirties was a very different place from the Charlbury of today. It was full of many characters, even at times a sleepy town, a great place to grow up in.

Harold Wakefield of Fulwell was also a pupil of Bill's:

> I attended Charlbury Central School until 1939 and I remember Bill Campbell as a very good, kindly teacher. He was a good disciplinarian, so you didn't play him up, but he was a bit lax sometimes and didn't always notice the bits of paper being flicked about the classrooms by rubber bands!

His lessons were always interesting. He had black hair then, and always wore silver-grey trousers with a sports jacket.

He was very keen on gardening and started up a school vegetable and flower garden. The everlasting flowers were hung up to dry in the shed and sold later for about threepence a bunch, the money probably going to school funds. There were a few beehives too, which belonged to the school and were used for our studies. Bill kept a close eye on our activities. We were given marks, but no prizes, for gardening. I remember one autumn sweeping leaves off the paths with my friend Cyril. On one side of the garden there was a tree, probably an ornamental crab, with bright red fruits. They looked tempting, so we decided to knock some down. Bill caught Cyril in the act and gave him a whack on his behind. Bill didn't like to see that sort of thing.

He took us for nature walks in Wigwell field to study birds and flowers. We enjoyed that because he was always so interesting. I remember a dinner hour prank in Wigwell bottom, when three senior boys caught a pony that was grazing there. They got it against a wall so that one of them could get up on the pony's back. One of the others then slapped the pony's bottom, and the boy fell off into a bed of nettles. They were late for afternoon school, reported to the headmaster and had to stand outside his study at break-time every day for a month. They were deprived of football, but not caned. Nobody was ever caned.

Many years later, in the autumn of 1969 or 1970 when I was employed as a forester on the Ditchley estate, I was working with two other men at Dean preparing ground for tree-planting. While at work, we heard the sound of a bird in distress and traced it to what we decided was a yellow wagtail with its legs stuck in some silty mud. Fluttering above was another wagtail, also in distress. We managed to capture the trapped bird and after cleaning its legs, we let it go. I remembered that Bill had said that yellow wagtails were summer migrants. 'Well' I said, 'they haven't all gone yet!' Fortunately, I bought a copy of the *Oxford Mail* a day or two later, and in Bill's weekly 'Nature Notes', he described the differences between the yellow wagtail and the grey wagtail. I realised that the bird we had rescued was really a grey wagtail, so I was saved from naming the bird wrongly when I told him the story.

The last time I saw him was before his accident. I had called to see him and after sharing a beer together, we walked round his garden.

On December 9th 1940 Bill took on the headmastership of Shipton-under-Wychwood school. From reading through the school log, it is clear it cannot have been an easy task. Leaving aside the sometimes poor attendance due to illness and bad weather, for many children came from scattered villages, the country was at war. Everyone was having to cope in often very difficult circumstances; there was rationing and a tension in the air and some families were suffering from the loss of loved ones. On arriving to take up his post, Bill found that one of the wooded school buildings had been set on fire during the night and certain items were missing about the place.

The weather was icy cold, with heavy falls of snow and blizzards and frozen pipes. The school rooms were sometimes no more than 35 degrees Fahrenheit. Bill could not get petrol to travel to work from Charlbury and sometimes walked, or took the train, which was unreliable. There were many frustrations. On occasions there was a lack of teachers, school milk and coal ordered did not arrive. Children were sometimes inadequately clad, and during a thaw many had wet feet and Bill provided them with PT slippers whilst they were in school. Evacuees swelled the numbers in the school and mumps and measles were prevalent. On the plus side, there were health visits with checks made on head lice and a dentist called on a regular basis. On 15th July, 98 children were immunised against diphtheria, which was followed up by a second immunisation on 12th August. Dr. Scott who sent coal to warm the place and offered the loan of his half-acre paddock for a school garden, was a wonderful support and the vicar was always available for advice.

In spite of the troubles Bill had to deal with, the school inspectors in 1941 were full of praise, which included the following words from the Rev. T.P. Backhouse, General Diocesan Inspector of church schools in Oxfordshire:

> Having known the acting Headmaster since 1927, I was particularly looking forward to visiting this school. My opinion, which I have held for some time, that he is a teacher of exceptional ability, was fully confirmed. He thoroughly understands the possibilities (which are many) of a country school, and he has the ability and energy to develop such a school on the best lines. Any country school would be fortunate to have him as headmaster.

But on February 27th 1949 Bill wrote in the school log book, 'This is my last day as headmaster of this school.' He had been appointed headmaster of the Mortimer Parochial School in Berkshire. Judy and Stuart Davey, in their book *Change at Cholsey Again!*, wrote that he brought

Bill Campbell with children from Cholsey Primary School, together with his wife May.

'with him a particular interest in nature and ornithology. He is best remembered by his pupils for his inspiring nature walks and the lasting knowledge he imparted on that and other subjects. His reputation as a naturalist grew as he wrote articles and books on the subject.' His wife, May, was one of his staff, and in 1970 they retired and came to live in Charlbury. From then on he was able to relax on the whole, and devote more of his time and attention to his great love for the countryside and its plants and animals. Another garden was to be made.

3

POETRY

Bill loved poetry. As a young man when living and working in London and far from the Cotswolds and the people he knew so well, he wrote this beautiful, though sad, poem.

Memory

When she was kind, oh all was fair,
Love – whispering trees, soft kissing air
With careless bliss seemed laden;
E'en when it rained I sensed no tear
(For love makes blackest clouds seem clear)
But thought o' my sweet maiden.

And I, well-pleased, in lightsome mood,
Would wander in calm solitude,
Amid a lonely maze of gorse,
Above where lazy Evenlode
Through hazy pastures wound its course.

The gorse-bloom smiled, the linnets sang.
The wild woodpecker's laughter rang,
As from a thorn, with dipping flight,
So that in turn he dived and swam.
Away he sped, a beauteous sight.

But yet I thought of little, save
Of her dark hair's soft-rippling wave,
The faithful brown of her clear eyes
(Like mountain streams where elfins bathe)
And that to me, by youthful ties

She did belong, and I to her;

Old-fashioned flowers our tokens were
Deep-blushing roses to convey
What first my tied tongue dared not say;
Rosemary for remembrance,
(She wore the sprig at that last dance)
And sweetly bold, pure sky-blue dot,
The straightforward Forget-me-not.

But now, though May-bloom scents the wind
It brings no solace to my mind,
For my beloved has left me,
And all around me seems unkind
Since heedless Fate bereft me.

For when I walk 'mid flowery beds
The roses lift their haughty heads,
And leering openly, they say
'Shall we go tell of love today?'
And Rosemary, sweet emblem once,
Shouts ruthlessly 'Remembrance!'
No signs of tokens need I now
To mind me of our mutual vow,
But to complete my misery
Small eyes of blue peep up at me,
And now the simpering, sky-blue dot
In mockery sighs, 'Forget her not.'

Oh still-beloved, I little thought
When such fond symbols I gave thee
That happiness may come to naught.
Now bitter-sweet is Memory!

In 1927 and living close to his much-loved Wychwood Forest, Bill recalled, 'It was an extremely memorable evening when I happened to go out into the garden just before sunset. Ducks were pouring overhead going to the lakes in Wychwood. The sun began to set and the sky was streaked with glorious colour which gradually deepened to even greater beauty. Starlings were coming to a big roost and I just went indoors and wrote this.'

Wychwood Nightfall

On whining wings wild duck speed overhead,
Their eager necks out-stretched towards the pines
Whose jagged blackness blots the fiery red,
Where midst tumultuous skies the day declines.

Soft rosy hues suffuse the forest's face;
As opal-breasted ring-doves roostward fly,
And all around the firs, their settling place,
Round silvery limbs the purple birch-twigs lie.

Belated from the fresh-ploughed fields afar,
The fluttering starlings haste in throbbing flocks;
Between the beech-boughs peeps the evening star;
Shrill-screaming vixen hails the barking fox.

From ivied elm and ancient hollowed oak
Brown owls come forth with quavering mournful hoot,
To call awake the wood's nocturnal folk;
A badger grunts beneath its lintel-root.

Bill once said,

'I'm old fashioned enough to have encouraged the older children I
taught, the upper forms, to learn poetry by heart. I remember two incidents
which illustrate the fact that children love poetry and don't care anything
about the sense, it's the sound and rhythm they like. One boy I recall, was
reciting in class part of Coleridge's dramatic *The Rime Of The Ancient
Mariner*, when he came to the verse,

> *All in a hot and copper sky*
> *The bloody sun at noon,*
> *Right up above the mast did stand,*
> *No bigger than the moon.*

The boy began

> 'All in a hot and copper sky
> The bloody sun at noon,
> Right up above the mast did stand
> And – er and – er – er – And so did the bloody moon!'

On another occasion a boy was reciting *Weathers* by Thomas Hardy, the last lines of which are,

> *And meadow rivulets overflow,*
> *And drops on gate-bars hang in a row,*
> *And rooks in families homeward go,*
> *And so do I.*

As he came to the end he got in a bit of a muddle, but it didn't matter, he went straight on.

> 'And meadow rivulets overflow,
> And rooks in families homeward go,
> And drops on gate bars hang in a row,
> And so do I!'

Bill also once recollected a story which inspired another of his poems:

About sixty years ago I met an old man in his seventies who was a stone-mason but also a great antiquarian, and I told him that the night before the keepers had caught a couple of poachers in the forest. 'Aye,' he said, 'poaching isn't what it used to be.' And he went on to tell me the story about how two chaps were caught poaching in the forest and accused of killing a keeper and were hanged. Then years later it turned out that someone else had shot the keeper and I always remember he finished up by saying, 'Owever, if them two had never been hung, them'd both be jed by now!' Anyway, the story impressed me so much, that that night in bed I made up this versification of his account and it went more or less like this. Oh, I must explain one or two things; a 'boy chap' was a teenager, to 'brevit' means to search about frantically, 'chep' is cheap, 'mate' is meat and 'fyern' is fern or bracken. So anyway, we'll begin.

> When I was a boy chap, that's three score year ago,
> The old lady I lodged wi' was seventy or so.
> Now when she was a wench she once 'eard a chap say
> As 'im and his mate knew where a buck lay,
> And having no money for beef steak nor chops,
> Them reckoned on chep mate from Tumpbury Copse.
> That was all she heard, 'twas nothing to she,
> But fearful things came on it as you will see.
> That same night when going home long Withey way,
> A mason hears groanings as nye turned him grey.

Then thinking for someone a bit markey merry
He brevits about in the fyern round Tumpbury.
But finds it was summat far worser than beer;
A keeper all bleeding he found lying there.
'Twas the poacher 'as done it,' the poor fellow said,
And them was his last words for soon he was jed.
Now this news put the wench in a terrible way,
But she witnessed at sessions to all she'd 'eard say.
At Oxford Assizes she said the same too
And Jason and Caleb the poachers says, 'True.
Us planned to go poaching and poaching us went
But of blood, saving deers' us both innocent!'
But the Judge dons his black cap and says very callous
'Tis plain as you two chaps must go to the gallous.'
Now when them 'ad been hung and forgot twenty year,
Old Jonathan Pratley was took very queer,
And feeling his chances of living were small
He sent for the Parson and then told him all.
How as on that sad night he had shot just for luck
At summat a-moving, as he thought was buck,
But was really the keeper awaiting for he.
Then Jonathan died groaning, 'Twernt them, 'twas me.'
Now, maybe you thinks this a very sad tale,
And in places it is, I allow,
However – if them two had never been hung,
Them 'ud both 'em be jed be now!

Bill made several recordings with Ken Jackson, who presented Natural History programmes on BBC World Service, and now runs his own audio company producing wildlife and countryside cassettes and CDs. In one of the cassettes, called *The Nature of Poetry*, Bill had some interesting points to make about some of the poems that were included:

> *Home-Thoughts From Abroad* has always been one of my favourites, but I can never understand why Browning only gave the thrush two repetitions of his song, you know, 'he sings each song twice over'. But I don't know why on earth he didn't say thrice, which would have been nearer the mark and it would have sounded exactly the same. The thrush will repeat his song three and four times, twice is rather exceptional. In my opinion, I don't think the bird is such a beautiful songster, it's lovely because it starts so early

in winter, but compared with a blackbird, it's not at all musical. I'm sure that the thrush in poetry gets an awful lot of credit that it doesn't really deserve, 'though I'm very fond of him!

Gillian Stone's poem, *Starlings in a Dying Oak*, I was very impressed with, because a lot of people have got a thing about starlings, they don't like them. I think chiefly because they predominate at bird tables and drive smaller birds away, but they're really beautiful birds in their spring plumage, they are extremely useful with the good they do, eating grubs and so on, and they are absolutely our most spectacular bird when they mass in winter at huge roosts. Now in this case, on this dead oak, I imagine this would be just a minor gathering of perhaps a few thousand, very impressive, but if you go to the final rendezvous, the real roosting place, you may get – I have tried estimating counting this – millions. Not only the phenomenal thing of vast numbers of a bird together, you get the marvellous sound from a great gathering like that and you get marvellous aerial evolutions before they actually pour into roost.

Now in Clare's poem *The Thrush's Nest*, there's the kind of thing that happens a lot in Clare, he uses some local expressions, names for things really, which puzzle people sometimes. I always remember reading some book about his poems, and they were assuming that when he refers to swifts he meant the birds, but it just didn't make sense. I happen to know that in East Anglia, a swift is a lizard and it made sense! This one too might puzzle people when he mentions heath-bells, and since he mentions they are the same colour as thrush's eggs, it's obvious they are harebells, the bluebells of Scotland.

About the poem by William Strode, *On Westwell Downs*, again it's evocative, because what seems to be stressed there is, 'the bareness of the turf all the year round'. In the early days when I became familiar with downland on the Berkshire Downs, that was the case, it was always short turf; marvellous with flowers in spring and summer, wonderful for nesting birds like stone curlew and wheatear and now of course it's all gone. There are two main reasons: in the old days, it was either sheep or rabbits that kept it lawn-like and then two things happened, one, myxomatosis, which reduced the rabbits and the other, the tractor replacing the horse, so that they could plough and cultivate right up to the top of these downs. So that now, the short downlands are almost a thing of the past, except with the notable innovation of Nature Reserve bodies, like our own Berks, Bucks and Oxon Naturalist Trust, where they are trying to recreate old downland conditions by running sheep on their Reserves.

4

RADIO AND *NATURE TRAIL*

When Bill retired in 1970 he and his wife May returned to Charlbury to live. Bill made one more garden, full of fruit trees and fruit bushes, vegetables and flowers, but this time there were no beehives.

In 1973 Bill took over the Radio Oxford *Nature Trail* programme from Dr. Bruce Campbell. This programme was inspired by one that went out during the war called *Rambling with Romany.* After the war when Bruce was working with the BBC in Wales, he recreated the same format. It entailed two children exploring the countryside once a week at all times of year, with a natural history expert to guide them. The difference with *Nature Trail* was that in the first two instances, the children never left the studio, as the equipment necessary for easy outdoor recording had not been invented, whereas this time with the development of tape and portable recorders the programmes really came from the great outdoors! So, in the early days, it was all scripted with a two hour rehearsal from a drama producer, and all the sounds added in the studio, either at the time of recording or later. We gather there were often tears from the children, for it wasn't much fun at times. Not so in *Nature Trail,* for the children were out in the countryside every time and never saw the inside of a studio (or a drama producer!), since all the programmes were unscripted and edited by the producer on his own in the studio later. These children had the added advantage of the wonderful companionship and knowledge of both Bruce and Bill. The programme ran for seven years, such was its success.

One glorious summer's day, early on in their recordings, Bill and the children – Jo and Doug – and their father, Ken, who recorded and produced all the programmes, visited White Horse Hill. Bill's wife, May, who was then an invalid, was sitting and waiting in one car and I – in my capacity as the youngsters' mother and the producer's wife – in another. It was my birthday and I took a bottle of wine over to May and told her what the celebration was and asked her if she would join me while we waited. She smiled as she agreed and told me it was their son Donald's birthday too. He had been the greatest possible joy to them and had grown up to be a talented, promising young man. Later, I was to find out for myself from photographs that he was also strongly built, and exceedingly good-looking. He played the saxophone and had his own band, which appeared on television.

He had just qualified as a dentist and was visiting his parents one day, when Bill received an invitation to write nature notes for the *Oxford Mail*. 'I think you ought to write for the *Oxford Mail*, Dad.' Donald said before he left in his car. There was black ice on the road and he got into a skid and was killed. Privately they never recovered from their grief, but publicly they carried on with their lives, filling the days with interest and consideration for others.

May and I sat together quietly celebrating the birthdays, remembering days that had gone and waiting for the broadcasters on the hill to finish. From that day, every July 20th until his death, Bill gave me a basket of fruit and a bunch of flowers from his garden.

May died at home very suddenly towards the end of 1974, and in time Sheila, one of Bill's sisters, who had just lost her husband, came to live with Bill. They were a comfort to each other and lived together in great harmony, until Sheila's death in hospital some years later.

He was alone again, but he kept himself as busy as ever. Among many other activities, continuing the weekly recordings for Radio Oxford's *Nature Trail*, which he had begun just before May's death, and when the series ended when the children became too old to sustain that format of programme, he contributed regularly to Radio Oxford's *Countrywise* and BBC World Service's *Nature Notebook*. So his words live on both in the radio archives and in the many recordings he has done for the Sounds Natural series of audio cassettes and CDs. His way with the spoken word is just as memorable as it is in his many writings, especially those for the *Guardian*'s 'Country Diary', excerpts from which appear in Chapter 9. Those who heard him 'in the flesh' will I'm sure relive the voice as they read excerpts from the transcriptions of two of over five years' worth of *Nature Trail* programmes he did with Jo and Dougie. First, from a programme transmitted in September 1974 when they went just outside Oxfordshire:

WD   Well here we are in rather a new place for Nature Trail, we're actu-
     ally in Northamptonshire, aren't we?

DJ   Yes.

WD   We've come near the canal and, do you know, when we were
     coming I was thinking if we get to some watery meadows, I wonder
     if there will be any so-and-sos, and there are. Now then it's up to
     you to find them ... amongst these cattle; on the grass there are
     some small birds, brownish with some yellow underneath, and
     when they move, as I hope they will in a minute, you'll see some
     whitish tail feathers. Who's going to spot the first one? I've seen
     three but I can't see one now.

JJ   Just behind the bull, is that one?

WD   Yes. Well now these, they don't look very yellow at present but they
     are yellow wagtails and why I thought we would see them is now
     they are gathering together because they are just going to leave. We
     have three wagtails, you know the common black and white, don't
     you?

DJ   Yes, the pied.

WD   And then there's the very long tailed one, which also is very, very
     yellow underneath, that's the grey wagtail and we've seen that by
     water sometimes – in summer and winter. But this yellow wagtail
     comes from Africa to nest here and of course will soon be going
     back. It likes wettish places and it likes following cattle, now can
     you guess why?

DJ   The cows stir up the grass.

WD   Yes, the cattle walking through the grass and plants disturb insects
     and the wagtails pounce on them.

DJ   Oh look, there's a water vole carrying some plant.

WD   Yes, it was carrying a piece of grass or rush in its mouth. There he
     goes look, he's got a little tunnel under that tuft of grass.

JJ   Oh, there's two of them.

WD   Yes, there are.

DJ   He's just submerged.

WD   Now there's a nice thing growing under our noses. You haven't got
     any nettle stings have you?

JJ/DJ No.

DJ   It's a dock!

WD Yes, but this is a special one, what do you notice about it?

DJ It's bigger.

WD Well it's huge and that's the great water dock. Very handy, that would cover a lot of nettle stings.

JJ Will we see any more water rats along this piece?

WD Well, there's not such a thing as a water rat you know. These poor things are nearly always called water rats and they're not, they are much nicer creatures than rats, they don't do any harm. They're voles – v o l e s – not moles, and they're harmless. I mean they don't come and …

DJ Bite you.

WD Rob food and do things like that, like real rats do. They're vegetarians, they just eat weeds along the edge of the water. They do burrow in the banks, but that doesn't cause much trouble.

JJ And also they don't look like rats at all.

WD No, they haven't got pointed noses, you see, and they haven't got sticking up ears.

Secondly from a Trail they did early on May Morning in 1974:

JJ White rabbits!

WD Well, I was looking at a heron going over, but still … . . Now why 'white rabbits'?

JJ Well we always say that at the beginning of the month.

WD Oh I remember. When I was a youngster it used to be supposed to be lucky to say 'rabbits' the first thing you spoke on the first day of the month, but I'd forgotten all about it. I think we'll say, 'Happy May Morning'.

JJ OK.

WD Now Jo, are you going to bathe your face in the dew to make yourself even more beautiful? I think you should, but there's only one thing I think I should warn you – it's rather frosty dew I think, because it's freezing … still I should do it just to say you've done it!

DJ Is it only girls who do it?

WD Well you can try and see if it'll have any effect on you, I don't think it will!

JJ I doubt it!

Bill Campbell with Doug and Jo Jackson, recording on White Horse Hill for Radio Oxford.

DJ   I've already washed myself this morning.

WD   It's a shame having to wash twice, before breakfast!

JJ   Why do you wash your face with dew?

WD   I don't really know Jo, I don't think anyone does. There are all sorts of superstitions connected with May and I don't think anyone knows how they began. I think it's a sort of celebration that summer's beginning, or ought to be beginning. I should think probably it's a very old festival – a heathen one. Easter was first of all you see a celebration of spring by heathen people and then it became connected up with Christianity, but I don't think May has any connection like that, I think it's purely and simply a sort of hope 'here's summer come at last'.

DJ   It's given us an excuse to get up early today.

WD   Do you need an excuse to get up early?

DJ   No, except for school!

WD   Well one thing about this morning, the cuckoo's been going for a long, long time. It greeted this May Morning very early.

DJ   Is that white blossom sloe?

WD   Yes it's the flowers of blackthorn, not – on this May Morning – not may. You know they call hawthorn blossom 'may', but may isn't out yet. It's hardly ever nowadays that you find hawthorn blossom, that is may blossom, out on May Morning, it's too early for it. It's rather a puzzling story for you I expect, but I think in the old days it used to be out because May Day used to come later – they altered the calendar 200 years ago you see, and put it on eleven days. So, in eleven days time you might just find hawthorn out.

DJ   They use 'mayday' to show you're in danger.

WD   Ah, that's the French '*m'aidez*', 'help me', but still it sounds the same.

DJ   Yes … have those dandelions not come out yet today?

WD   They haven't come out yet but yesterday they would have been wide open. They're still asleep in fact. Lots of people who don't get up early don't notice this. A tremendous number of flowers go to sleep at night, so to speak, and shut up their petals, and if you look at the clover in the grass there, the clover leaves do the same – they fold right up you see, fold up and backwards.

DJ   Oh yes, they look a bit frosted.

WD   Well, they are, just coated with frost, it hasn't hurt them.

JJ   Why do they do it – fold up, I mean?

WD   I think it's to prevent loss of heat at night and perhaps with flowers it's to protect them from the cold. I think it prevents them losing moisture as well.

5

RINGING FOR THE BTO

When Bill reached sixty years of bird ringing in 1991, he was asked by the British Trust for Ornithology to ponder on those years. It had been more than forty years since he had pioneered the use of insect and fruit baits in chardonneret traps to catch warblers – long before the introduction of the all-pervasive mist-net.

In 1930 I joined the Oxford Ornithological Society. Eminent members of that body then were Bernard Tucker and Wilfred Alexander, and both of these were my early mentors. I am particularly indebted to the latter, who became a lifelong friend and frequent field-companion, for suggesting that I should become a ringer. This I did, at first confining my activities to nestlings. Two years later, I made my first of many subsequent visits to Skokholm, where I was introduced to ringing on a large scale.

I recall that on one visit, when Wilfred Alexander was also there, he frowned upon the current practice of merely 'squashing' the soft Witherby rings on to the legs, and ahead of his time, suggested that there was a need for special pliers for the operation.

But two most important developments in my ringing activities occurred when, after the death of my father, the family moved to Wychwood village a few miles away. Here I found that 'clap netting' of birds roosting in the hedges was still a local sport, most of the captures ending up as ferret food, apart from robins and wrens, which were released. The practitioners of this activity readily allowed me to accompany them, and were soon converted to my less lethal objective – as one of them remarked, on stroking a redwing which I was ringing, 'You be a lucky little bugger – once upon a time us 'ould 've wringed your neck – now Mr Campbell is only going to ring your leg!'

This activity, from late August onward throughout the winter, resulted in bags of a wide variety of species, often 30 or 40 per night. The first recovery abroad, that of a winter-ringed blackbird found nesting in Denmark in the following spring, impressed my helpers greatly.

The 'clapper', who walked slowly down the hedge with the net extended, whilst the 'lusher' on the other side beat the hedge with a long stick and I shone an acetylene lamp on to the nets, had once asked me how much it would be worth if he caught a bird which I could not name. Rashly in those good old pre-decimal days, I risked half-a-crown. One night, when attempting to catch high-roosting fieldfares, Norman clapped the poles together and shouted, 'Here's my first half-crown!' But, thanks to a memory of the plates in John's book, I was able to say casually (despite inward excitement) 'Oh, it's a great grey shrike'.

The second boost to ringing activity, came when an elderly neighbour brought me a somewhat worm-eaten chardonneret trap – of the original type with two compartments, the lower of which held the captive decoy-bird. She told me that, as a little girl (which must have been about 70 years before) she had used the trap, baited with suet, to catch tits.

I removed the lower portion, and with a strip of rubber from an old inner-tube as motive power, converted the top to my first of many chardonnerets. Noticing that a willow warbler was hovering to pick off mealy aphids from the underside of plum leaves, I set the trap in the tree baited with upside down leaves, to facilitate exploitation, and immediately caught the bird. Noticing also that various warblers – willow, whitethroats and blackcaps – were picking off the red currants and the daphne berries, I baited traps with these, again with immediate results, and thus began an interest into what natural foods were preferred by garden visitors.

More traps were constructed and used with such baits, and it soon indicated that many of the so-called insectivorous migrants, especially blackcaps, lesser whitethroats and garden warblers, showed a marked preference for succulent berries, during the period of their availability, say from late July until late September, whilst others, notably whitethroats and willow warblers, revealed an appetite for both fruit and insects, with no marked bias to one or the other. The one outstanding insectivorous warbler was the chiffchaff, but even this was occasionally attracted to berries.

To confirm what was merely a general impression as to these preferences, I decided, when my battery of traps had grown to 44, on a more scientific approach. Whenever both berries and insects, the latter mainly aphids and the green caterpillars of the small white butterfly, were equally available, I baited traps, set mainly in rows of peas on sticks, alternately with each other, and kept records of the results. An extreme example of preference demonstrated by this approach occurred once, when I had set about twenty traps in several rows of peas, and soon afterwards had a catch of seven lesser whitethroats, each in a berry-baited trap, whilst the insect baited traps had been disregarded.

On moving to Berkshire, in two separate locations in 28 years, I was fortunate on each occasion to find that my garden seemed to be on a main route for post-breeding dispersal, particularly for warblers. So it was that in one, near a large copse, in one season in a very small garden, I ringed 244 whitethroats and 166 willow warblers. In this particular site my plums, especially a delicious greengage, were relished by lesser whitethroats, but my usual technique of baiting traps with prime specimens failed to achieve the desired result. After prolonged spells of watching, I solved the problem – the birds only attacked fruits which had already had their skins broken by tits or wasps, and thereafter, I simply prepared the baits by gashing the skin with my thumb-nail, with positive results. Even a confirmed insect-eater, the spotted flycatcher, may, in adverse weather conditions just prior to departure, turn to fruits in the absence of insects, and once, in a rainy spell, I caught seven in traps baited with berries of red currants and honeysuckle – and once, accompanied by Eric Ennion, watched one feeding on yew berries.

In my present site, only a mile or so from where it all began, but in more open country, far fewer birds pass through my garden, and although the chardonnerets catch winter-visiting siskins (with interesting recoveries – mainly indicating Scottish origin, but also one controlled in the next May in Norway), mist-nets alongside a hedge in a field, just across the lane from my house, provide the bulk of my catches. So far I have ringed around 60,000 birds of 110 different species, but, apart from recoveries in almost every European country, and in Morocco, Israel and the Congo, I have derived most satisfaction from my investigations into the food preferences of garden visitors.

I must finish with two records which may be unique; once, in Connemara, a brood of twites exploded from a fuchsia hedge, and I extracted one from the curly mop of my niece and ringed it. The old Witherby rings arrived loose in a packet, and it was my practice to thread each size on sticks of the appropriate calibre and carry them in a cigarette case. Once, for some unknown reason, I had transferred these to my shirt-pocket before a cricket-match, and, as captain (not for any prowess with either bat or ball) I had placed myself in a very rough outfield, and during a lull in the proceedings, realised that I was standing over a brood of skylarks, which were duly ringed.

Bill at home in his garden.

As a tribute to Bill's enormous ringing efforts and successes, Chris Mead of the British Trust for Ornithology wrote this in *The Guardian*:

The Lord of the Ringers

William Campbell, the *Guardian*'s Country Diarist in Oxfordshire since 1964, spent more than 60 years ringing birds and was one of the longest serving ringers ever under the national bird-marking scheme. More than 60,000 birds of an amazing 110 species were marked and the results of his marking broke new frontiers.

His interest was first kindled by eminent members of the Oxford Ornithological Society, which he joined in 1930, and it was Wilfred Alexander who suggested he should take up ringing. At that time the scheme was organised by Harry Witherby, the publisher of *British Birds*, and not yet the British Trust for Ornithology – founded a few years later by many of the same enthusiasts of the Oxford OS.

To start off he used techniques like 'bat-fowling', where birds roosting in hedges were gathered in with two hinged nets, a method still used by country folk to catch blackbirds for the pot or to feed the ferrets. A great breakthrough followed when an elderly neighbour gave him a chardonneret trap made out of wire netting – used 70 years previously for catching finches for caging. He adapted the design to use modern materials like inner-tube and was in business. Not only were the readily baited birds, like greenfinches and tits, caught but he realised that other far less easily caught birds could be trapped with the right bait.

This proved amazingly effective. Willow warblers came for mealy aphis on the underside of plum leaves. Red currants and *Daphne mezereum* berries proved irresistible to blackcaps and whitethroats in the late summer with elderberries, raspberries and blackberries taking over later in the autumn. Caterpillars were offered in traps for the more insectivorous species like chiffchaffs, and even spiders' webs proved a useful lure – for spotted flycatchers in nest-building mood. About 10 years ago WD (or to some Bill and others Donald) gave a fascinating talk on birds and berries at the annual ringers' conference when he ran out of time and was called back the next year to finish.

His favourite warbler was the lesser whitethroat. These he caught on plums, particularly greengages, in chardonnerets. The skin had to be broken and this was achieved by gashing the skin with his thumbnail. His success in catching the birds was rewarded by the first report from abroad of a lesser whitethroat from Britain – a juvenile bird ringed in 1954 and found the following April in Israel.

In 1959 he had another recovery, but in autumn and from Italy; a 1966 juvenile provided our second report, late in the following March, in Israel again. Now there are almost 100 recoveries abroad indicating a movement in autumn through northern Italy and the Nile Delta to the wintering area in the highlands of Ethiopia. Return passage in spring is through the Near East and Cyprus. But 20 years ago three of the 25 recoveries we had on file had come from the dedicated ringing in that Cholsey garden of a remark-able all-round naturalist.

Bird-watching has become a competitive sport for many of its practi-tioners so that numbers and rarity mean everything. WD delighted in the seasonal changes he recorded, in the ebb and flow of migrants, and indeed in rarities. However they were never the ultimate passion for him. It was the observation of nature in familiar places, the garden, the Forest, Farmoor Reservoir or his beloved Scotland.

In the summer of 1986 he had a fall during one of his regular visits to Portland Bill – he was with the warden, Mick Rogers, in the dark and on the rocks on a night-time session ringing storm petrels. He insisted on staying until the first bird was caught – his first handling of this elusive species – then consented to be taken to hospital to have the broken ribs treated. He agreed to remain in hospital another night only when Mick Rogers promised there would not be another petrel-ringing session.

Chris Mead

6

WYCHWOOD AND CORNBURY

Bill was associated with Wychwood Forest from 1910 until his death in 1994. He had permission to go anywhere on the estate at any time, so that even when he went to teach in Berkshire for 21 years, he used to come down in spring, summer, autumn and winter and walk in the forest, noting the changes as time passed. Part of the forest eventually became a National Nature Reserve, and Bill was for a long time a voluntary warden. Looking back over the years with all its changes, Bill's memories and knowledge of the history of place are both intriguing and interesting. The following are selections from recordings made of Bill's lectures and some remembered conversations over a period of years.

The area which is known as Wychwood is not known as that to the locals, because everyone I know never talks about Wychwood, it's always The Forest. In the old days it seemed always to be referred to as Cornbury and as far as we know Cornbury Forest or Wychwood Forest was a royal hunting ground even in the time of William the Conqueror and probably, almost certainly, in Saxon times before. There must have been houses of some sort there, but the first record of a stone-built house at Cornbury was 1337. In 1383 the Park was enclosed by a wall – the old feudal term was that it was 'emparked' – and it became an official fallow deer park. Henry I in the early 1100s actually stayed at what house there was at Cornbury and he apparently was very interested in wildlife, because he had a zoo at Woodstock at which there were bears and all sorts of odd things which didn't occur at Wychwood.

One of the occasions I visited Cornbury house itself, was at Christmas time, when at about five in the morning, I would go with my father to help decorate what we called the 'Big House' with holly and ivy and all the other things. I remember that in the big stone hall, which was a great entrance place to Cornbury House, there were pictures with blinds over them. Dad used to pull the blinds up and show me and say, 'Now Willy, this is a marvellous picture, it's an Old Master and worth thousands of pounds.' Little did he know that when the estate was sold up, it wasn't thousands of pounds, it was millions!

In the sixteenth century the house was inhabited by the Earl of Leicester in Queen Elizabeth's reign. The place did not belong to him, he was looking after it for someone else. He was a great favourite and would-be husband of Queen Elizabeth, and Cornbury became famous because he met his death there. There is still a Leicester Room and if you visit it, you will see blood stains on the floor, so they say, but I believe he was poisoned, though nobody really knows. When we children were living in Wychwood, we were told the forest was haunted by Amy Robsart. She was the wife of the Earl of Leicester and she also met a mysterious death by falling downstairs, not at Cornbury, but at Cumnor, but how she came to haunt Cornbury Forest, I don't know.

When we get to the time of Charles I the house became the gift of his friend, Lord Danvers. A new face was added on to the old Tudor part, facing the forest onto what's now the Grand Vista, the south-west aspect of the place. An interesting fact is that this was devised and carried out by a local stonemason, Nicholas Stone, appropriately. I think he came from Taynton. At the same time Lord Danvers established the Botanic Gardens in Oxford and Nicholas Stone made the marvellous gateway that leads into them.

In the next reign of Charles II, it came into the hands of another Royal favourite, Lord Clarendon. His name was Hyde and he built the splendid south-facing aspect of Cornbury House that you see from the direction of Stonesfield. It is interesting to note that this Lord's granddaughter became Queen Anne.

In the middle of the eighteenth century the Spencer family, the Spencer Churchills, were at Cornbury, and the Duke of Marlborough as he was then bought Cornbury for his son, who was the Marquis of Blandford, so for a short time it became Blandford Park, not Cornbury. However the old name was eventually restored. Then about the middle of the nineteenth century, Queen Victoria visited her favourite lady-in-waiting, Lady Churchill, at Cornbury and Charlbury, the market town close by, has a fountain that was built to commemorate the Queen's visit.

In the forest there is the Iron Well, to which the Ordnance Survey people give the grand name of Chalybeate spring. About four yards away there is an old stone seat. One Palm Sunday I was showing a group of people round as Voluntary Warden for the Nature Conservancy and I said,

'You see that old stone seat over there, once many years ago, Queen Victoria sat on that and had a drink from the Iron Well.' There were some yobs in the group and whether the one who made the following remark was a nitwit or a witty bloke I don't know, but he looked at the Iron Well and looked at the seat and said, 'My God, 'er must have had a long neck!'

In about 1857 it became a private estate and was no longer a Royal Forest and things altered. It was bought by a man named Du Cros and after that it was bought by the Watney family, Vernon Watney and Lady Margaret Watney, who became interested in local affairs. Lady Margaret was the daughter of the Earl of Portsmouth. She found out that I was interested in flowers and used to encourage me, sometimes arranging for me to show some of her visitors the forest flowers.

In Watney's time, you could regard the gardens at Cornbury as those of a stately home. It was a very well kept-up estate with a garden of four acres surrounded by a very tall wall, stone on the outside and brick on the inside, so that the fruit trees could be trained all the way round it. The garden was divided up into four sections, which was typical of that time – it had been walled in 1680. There were figs, peaches, apricots, pears, plums and so on and the garden employed 15 men, three of whom were resident. There was a large range of greenhouses and one of the most interesting things was that we grew bananas. There was one greenhouse full of banana plants grown in tubs and they would ripen here, not weeks ago in the West Indies and having come over here in the green state. I've never liked sharp bananas since.

One of the great changes on the estate has been that now there are only a man and a boy seeing to the garden and most of the greenhouses have been pulled down. In the old days the estate must have employed hundreds of people. I said there were 15 in the garden, and there were a lot of foresters and a lot of carters, and there were any amount in the big house itself, and there were of course a lot of keepers. One great feature of the forest used to be that many of its sections were what we call copses, and what the books call coppices, and if you look at an appropriate map you will still see that the forest is still named in many, many sections as Hazlewood Copse, Knightons Copse, Buckley Copse and so on. In those days the copse trees were hazel and every so many years, I suppose every ten years or so, they were cut down to ground level and grew again, but in between them – they weren't pure copses, they weren't just cleared – there were what we called 'copses with standard'. There were standard trees, mainly oaks or ashes, which were left to grow for hundreds of years, presumably, and in those conditions – with light being let in every ten years or so and then gradually closing over – you had a totally different flora or fauna from what you get today.

I think coppicing stopped during the last war, and today of course everything is grown together and is closed up and there's no light that gets to the ground. In the old days in the copses, you could get a marvellous variety of flowers – orchids, primroses – but particularly birds. Those are the sorts of conditions that suit many, many birds admirably and many flowers too. One of the chief birds that lived in the copse, was the nightingale and I could lie in bed with my window open at home and listen to at least seven separate ones singing.

The other big changes that have happened have been more or less accidental, although someone was responsible for them in the beginning. In my boyhood red squirrels abounded in the forest and they were so plentiful that since our doors were hardly ever shut or locked, one used to come in regularly after puss had gone out and left something on her plate, and finish off the scraps. Then somewhere in the late 1920s, grey squirrels appeared and almost immediately the reds started to disappear and grey squirrels became a pest. I can remember accompanying some of the workmen home to Leafield, helping to gather nuts, and you would simply go into one of these hazel copses when they were ripe and shake the trees and hazel nuts would shower down, and they would fill their baskets and you would fill your pockets. Now I doubt whether you will find a ripe hazelnut in the whole forest, because for some reason the grey squirrels attack them when there is a mere embryo kernel in them, and you will see them all chewed up and on the ground as soon as they begin to form.

For the last 600 years or so the park has been enclosed as a deer park with fallow deer, and deer have been there ever since. In my time living there, you would not see a fallow deer in the forest; if you did, you would report it to the keepers and they would be out in force and bump it off – they didn't want deer in the forest. They used to be abundant there when it was a Royal Forest, but when it became private, purchased by Lord Churchill somewhere in the early 1850s, one of the first things he did was to have all the deer eliminated from the forest, because of the trouble with poachers.

I have discovered that deer have a thing about orchids. They're supposed to be aphrodisiac – I don't know if that's why the deer like them or not – but time after time since I have been back, I've found that as soon as the orchid blooms start to come up, even before the petals open, nine years out of ten the deer will strip them right off.

The deer are bred there now, they kill a few hundred every year, and make a bit of money out of it. I think it costs quite a lot to shoot a deer – you have to come from Germany or Saudi Arabia to do it – and still they are a plague. Heaps of good orchid sites, where various marsh orchids and the like are to be found, get completely stripped by the deer nearly every year. The same problem has been found in other nature reserves.

To me, one of the most annoying changes is that in the middle of the forest, there was a big open area known as the Plain; it's still there, but is not what it used to be. In the old days, as far as I know, it had never been broken by the plough, and the flora there of lime-loving plants was marvellous. I used to consider it was as good as White Horse Hill, which is one of my great favourite flower places. There would be bee orchids, pyramidal orchids, rock-rose, thyme, clustered bellflower, all typical chalk and lime-loving plants in abundance – but then of course during the war, it was all ploughed up, fertilised and now it's only grass again.

But there is a very interesting thing that always puzzled me about the Plain. Apparently it's been there from time immemorial as an open space. Now normally you would expect it would revert to scrub and eventually to forest, and it didn't. I can remember once taking a party of Nature Conservancy people, naturalists, biologists, around there, and knowing I had known it for a long time, they said, 'Oh, Mr Campbell, in your days, what animals did they put on the Plain to graze it?' and I said, 'None.' 'Well, why didn't it revert to scrub?' I couldn't think, and after we had been walking around for a mile or two talking about other things, I suddenly remembered that in my time, every autumn, the owner, Mr Watney, used to burn the thatch off it and so of course shrubby plants never regenerated, but I don't think that had been going on before he came there in 1901, and what kept it as a plain for hundreds of years before, I don't know, except that it must have been grazed in some way.

One thing I must stress – it's what for years I've tried to ram into children's heads – don't believe anything just because you've seen it printed in black and white. I've been annoyed many times by reading references to Wychwood containing absolute rubbish. One of them was that there used to be a forest fair dating from I think twelve hundred and something, Henry III, where there were cattle and all sorts of things on the Plain and in the forest. They've got muddled up of course with the Charter granted to Charlbury for its market every Monday and then a longer fair at another time of the year. There was a forest fair, and it was a terrific affair in the end, but it wasn't ancient and it was nothing to do with marketing animals. What happened was that somewhere in the early 1800s, some local Methodists (there were Boltons from Finstock and Earlys, the blanket people from Witney, amongst them, I know) were disgusted with the carrying-ons at Witney Feast and they held a counter meeting, a picnic and prayer meeting, I suppose you could call it, on the Plain in Wychwood. That went on for a few years and eventually speculators moved in and brought in stalls to sell food and drink. This went on for years until finally Lord Churchill had to stop it because of the crime and carrying-ons that were going on there, but it was not an ancient fair. When we were living there, at about Witney Feast time (incidentally Witney Fyeast) a party would come and ask Mum if she would boil a kettle for them to make a cup of tea; they were a group of Methodists from Witney keeping up the old tradition – that's the last remnants of the forest fair taking place in the park just outside our house.

You'll find in the forest various deep openings now overgrown, which were obviously quarries once. I think the oldest quarry must have been the one from which the building in the 1300s was made. I can remember in one of them, which I think must have been one of the originals, perhaps for the fourteenth century building, there were several recesses and I used to poke about in them. One recess went right back and was perfectly dry. There was a nest there made of sticks as thick as my forearm. I can only think it was the remnants of a raven's nest. The last raven was killed in this area near Burford in about 1888, but in dry conditions such a nest would last forever.

The quarry that you pass without noticing unless you know where to look, is on the new footpath just past the sawmill, which to us was the saw pit. Just to the right there are the remains of a quarry that was once the main quarry, from which a lot of Cornbury House, the facing stone of Blenheim and a great deal of the Guildhall in London were built. So it is a very interesting quarry, which at this time is being used as a dump. I'll say no more.

Another interesting fact going back to my boyhood, is the names of a lot of the workmen. So many of them were Old Testament names, and I don't know why. I can remember, Noah Holifield, Levi Wiggins, Joshua Busby, Uriah Hut, Joby Franklin, Solomon Honeybone, Jason Franklin, Amos King. The only female name I can recall connected in that way is Naomi.

It is interesting to note how little things can change big things. I've mentioned the impact that the intrusion of deer into the forest has made on the flora, particularly orchids. I've mentioned how the invasion by grey squirrels not only ousted our good old native red squirrels, but also stopped hazel nut crops from developing. Now I've just come across a third very significant change that has happened through the introduction of an alien. It's not very important today, but in the old days when commoners had the rights of pannage, that is they could put their pigs and cattle in the forest at times when there was a fall of mast, such as beech nuts and acorns and things like that, it would have been very important if this event had happened then. Although there are any amount of oaks in the forest, you would be very hard put to find an acorn, which seems odd. What has happened is this. You can look under oak trees and you will find instead of acorns, the cups of acorns distorted with a little hole in the middle, but with no acorn in it. Oak trees are peculiar in that they are the hosts to a vast number of parasites, which are nearly all very minute species of wasps which form galls. They lay their eggs in the buds and the subsequent growth is distorted and forms in some cases oak apples, big soft spongy growths, or the hard oak marble galls, or bunches like currants, currant galls, or flat ones which are called spangle galls, or a sort of fuzzy one called pineapple gall.

The oak is famous for being the host to a great number of these parasitic galls caused by wasps, but it doesn't affect them, they don't seem to mind, they still go on flowering and producing acorns. But in the 1970s a new gall wasp suddenly appeared from the continent. It lays its eggs in the flower bud of the oak, which then starts to develop, but instead of producing a cup with an acorn, it distorts the cup and no acorn forms. If this goes on and on like this, there will be no regeneration of oaks whatsoever. The interesting thing is that lots of these gall wasps have alternate generations. For instance, the one that makes the spangles, the flat gall on oak leaves, at one stage of its life makes galls on the roots, and it goes like this, roots to leaves. Another one is rather different, as it has two different plants for its hosts. One is the turkey oak, it grows on that and then when the wasps hatch and fly, they go and produce a generation on our pedunculate oak. The turkey oak, which is abundant in the forest, is easy to distinguish from the others, because it has a very tough leaf and its acorn is fuzzy, the cup has bristles all over it. It was introduced here from Turkey about 200 years ago. It is no good for timber, but the real point is that if there were no turkey oaks, there would be none of this wretched pest and we should have acorns once again in this area. I was with my old pal, a great naturalist, Ted Ellis, in Norfolk and we found turkey oak there and the year afterwards I found some in Hook Norton at the Railway Nature Reserve and since then it has spread everywhere.

The Second World War made its mark at Cornbury. The park was simply filled with all sorts of transport, lorries, jeeps, tanks and it was then that the deer escaped from the park and got into the forest doing untold damage. There are rumours that there are thousands and thousands of army spares that were just disposed of and buried in the park. I know that when they cleared a site some years ago, they found an American jeep. I don't think there was a skeleton in it, although some would have it there was.

Right on top of the highest point of the forest at High Lodge, there's a moat; where the water comes from is a mystery. In days gone by rain water was our only water supply. In times of drought, we had to go down to the farm, on Crown land, not Cornbury land, down below Kingstanding, a name suggestive of ancient hunting, perhaps the King was King John? Anyway, at Kingstanding water was laid on, we'd go down with a couple of buckets and we always used to notice it tasted very resinous of pine trees. Some time afterwards we had the right to go in the forest to get dead wood from fallen trees and I came across a miniature gravestone with nothing on it except a crown and VR and later I found yet another. I asked the Cornbury agent about it and he looked up the records, but could find no reference to these stones. My theory is that some time in Queen Victoria's reign, since that's a damp part of the forest, water must have been laid on there from the pine trees to the valley to Kingstanding Farm and that's why that water tastes of resin. The buildings at Kingstanding have VR and a Crown on them and so there's the connection.

In the old days one of the favourite and cheapest sweets you could buy was 'Spanish', which was simply liquorice. You could buy a thousand strips of Spanish, which was like a ribbon of black liquorice. But for Spanish liquor, you had the bitter unsweetened medicinal liquorice, which you bought from the chemist in sticks, something like seaside rock. The chemists at Charlbury and Witney, used to stock up with it before Palm Sunday, because there was such a demand for it. So you would have this medicinal liquorice and you would buy usually the brown boiled peppermints and you made a concentrated solution at home of peppermint and liquorice. Then on Palm Sunday, the real tradition was that you took it down to this special sacred spring, wassal, or ussal, and topped it up with that, and that was Spanish liquor. It was never called Palm Sunday, it was Spanish Liquor Day. Years ago I met an old Leafield man and I said, 'Does anyone still still make Spanish liquor?' He put his hand in his pocket and produced a bottle and said, 'Have a top of that.' That was an old greeting I remember you had when you went into a pub. Recently I found another person who still made Spanish liquor, and I asked, 'Did you make it from wassal?' and he replied, 'Me Mum made it from the tap.' So it wasn't genuine! Nobody knows the connection with Palm Sunday, but Kibble reckons it was an old Christian habit. I should think it predates Christian times and was probably a heathen spring celebration. The interesting fact that wassal or ussal is 'worts well', and wort was Anglo Saxon for a herb and it was probably some herbal spring drink made from it.

The rights of access have survived, but apparently Lord Rotherwick tried to put a stop to it when he bought the estate and he found he couldn't. I don't think there's anything written, but it's a long established tradition that cannot be ended. There are one or two other traditions. Leafield people have the right to go in the forest on a Tuesday to get dead wood and Finstock and Ramsden people have it on another day. The right to gather dead wood was granted to Finstock by the Watney family in 1918.

Another error which I have come across in a book, is that in Cornbury Park there was a grove of ancient yew trees, among which the poet Addison would love to muse. He used to stay at Cornbury, but it was to Wychwood he went, to spend time in deep thought in the company of the ancient yews. If you know the forest, you may know the area behind what was always called the saw pit, now called the saw mill, where there are the remains of a very old quarry. There are great mounds there, I suppose the spoil from the original digging, and each one of them was crowned by a huge yew tree and the roots were all over the top like octopods. It was a marvellous place, absolutely dark even in summer, and I used to go there to swot long before I knew that Addison used it. The yews must have been hundreds of years old; the first part of the big house at Cornbury having been built in Tudor times, I should think they dated from then. One of the first things I did when I returned after being away some time, was to visit my old yew grove in the forest, but the trees had been cut down. You can sell yew wood by the pound, I believe, and if you are a millionaire every penny counts.

The only evidence of much human occupation I found on the Plain was when my father every year used to send some of the men to dig up so much turf, which was taken back and stacked for a year or two for loam for garden soil. The only things dug up were clay pipes, or remnants of clay pipes and I don't think they can all have been discarded while they were being smoked. I remember at Charlbury Club, they had clay pipes to throw at or shoot at. I think they would probably be from stalls used for that sort of thing, because they were made for next to nothing, and although poaching and legitimate shooting must have gone on in the forest for hundreds of years, it's extraordinary how little archaeological evidence there is by way of things actually found.

Now, apart from one complete clay pipe and hundreds and hundreds of fragments of clay pipe, about the only other thing I ever found was a medieval fishtail arrow head, which had a very, very sharp razor edge inside, more likely to cause damage hitting a deer than the usual barbed one and not so likely to stick in and not be able to be got out. Now this is interesting too, because in one of old John Kibble's books, there is a mention that down by Newel Pond in some old records, there used to be a mill, which is rather odd because there are only little tiny streams there, but of course they could dam them up, but it might have been a horizontal mill, not a vertical one.

But anyway, there they used to dig clay in the old days. I was along there one day when workmen were digging and two interesting things happened. One, they exposed a wall of nice dressed stone, which had been from some substantial building. While they were digging out the topsoil, lo and behold! I said, 'What's that?'

'Oh, only a rusty bit of iron.' It was this lovely fishtail arrow head! In Mr Watney's book, a huge tome, mainly devoted to the families that lived at Cornbury, there is a reference to some feuding between rival parties of gentlemen (so-called) from different parts of Wychwood, who had a clash over hunting rights and amongst other weapons they used were forked arrows, this may have been one of them.

One very vivid memory from the days that we lived at Cornbury, was that you could always tell when it was going to rain, because you could hear the Witney hooter. In those days the blanket factories had hooters. I think the morning one was at eight o'clock, and if you could hear it you knew it was going to rain. Of course that is a thing of the past now.

Here's a very interesting thing that shows the changes that can happen in a little fraction of a lifetime and what brings them about. The first workman's outfits I can remember were corduroy trousers, always gaiters, which were what we called leather leggings, heavy boots of course, and all the workmen had a shoulder bag, called a frail. If you remember the old fish baskets, it was a weave like that, but a much broader basket with webbing straps that went over the shoulder. It contained their grub and drink for the day. Their boots of course were hobnail and the interesting thing is, they never called them boots, they were shoes. But I have heard them referred to by the old English plural 'shoen'. Then after the First World War, subtle changes began to happen. The frails, the straw baskets, disappeared and the men wore army surplus haversacks. Gaiters disappeared, they now wore army surplus puttees they had been used to during the war. Little things like that to me are very interesting.

Another thing that's gone (and I'm afraid for ever) is at the Finstock end of the forest and also between the boundary of the forest and Chilson, where there used to be extensive heaths and patches of acid sandy soil. At Finstock they were great because of ling – oh, when I was a kid, shoulder high – and gorse; then of course when I come back after turning my back for just thirty years, it's a plantation of conifers and of course it's been fertilised and I don't think the heather will ever come back again. It is an example of what the ecological effect of that has been.

In those days I remember walking through the heather at night or even dusk and being scared stiff by what I thought was a hawk following me, hovering around my head all the time. I eventually learned it was a nightjar, and as I was walking through the heather and bracken, I was disturbing moths and this bird was taking advantage of it. Now nightjars are extinct round here, because there is no heath and they must have heathland.

7

MORE WYCHWOOD WORDS AND DIALECTS

As he often said, Bill loved words and their structure. Here are some more of his own, taken from lectures and recordings, about some words themselves.

Now I was talking about the people who worked on the estate. They came from all around, there would be a troop coming from Leafield, another lot from Finstock and some more from Chilson and a few from Charlbury and so on. As a five-year-old coming from school in Ireland, I at first spoke with an Ulster accent and suddenly came across this strange language which 'the men' as we always called them used, it was almost like a foreign language. I've discovered since that it was a grammatical language, there were certain things that were never said and some that were always said. Let's give you an example of what happened once.

On weekdays the garden boy, he was the lowest in the scale, used to go and get our milk from South Hill across the park and the river, but on Sundays we had to go ourselves and we usually settled the bill with the dairyman, Ben Hicks. There was a time when I had my cousin Ralph staying up from London, a bit older than myself, and one Sunday we walked to the dairy together. There was Ben and we went to pay the bill and he got a bit of paper, looked around and turned to my cousin and said, ''As thee gotta bitta cedar?' Ralph just gaped as if it was a foreign language. Now Ben Hicks was saying, 'Hast thou ever a piece of cedar?' Cedar was the old name for pencil, though it's made from juniper.

I remember once some men talking about Witney Feast and one of them said to the other, 'Bist thee going to Witney Feast?'

'Well, I donna whether I should go or not you,' was the reply. Then he turned to another and said, 'Thee shalln'st not go shalln'st thou?'

They didn't know what to do about w's, sometimes they stuck them in and sometimes they left them out. They talked about an old 'omen 'ooding in the forest. But, in some cases a 'w' was stuck in, a post was a pwost, but better still and almost in the language of Chaucer, a pwosty; a boy was a bwoy, and if he was a teenager he was a bwoy-chap. A coat was a cwoat and as well as sticking in w's, they used to stick in y's, and so a cat became a cyat and a gate became a gyate and a cart became a cyart and so on. They also left out h's and stuck a 'y' on instead and so you put a yat on your yead and you wouldn't eat anything you y-ated. Hearing the words used by the men on the estate which seemed peculiar to them, fired my interest in words, which has remained with me all my life, enjoying the crosswords of either the *Guardian* or the *Observer*, which I do every morning. There were some words I remember as a youngster, which though strange to me, I had to get used to. Always if you went for shelter, say you got against a tree when the wind was blowing, you would say you were in the burra. If wood was going a bit rotten, it was doracky. If bread was getting stale, it was cherky. If fruit was going off, it was racksy. I always remember one garden boy, a very nice chap too, who said to me once, 'You've got your bananas and peaches and grapes and so on,' he said, 'but you know what? Give I a racksy pear.'

Then there were words for movements, which we used quite a lot. If you crept up to anything silently, you sleered up to them and if you searched about in a hurry, you scrobbled. If you rushed about here and there, you scoorted about and if you searched diligently, you bretherted. If a thing was chancey, it was casalty – it was connected with casualty, so there's some point in it, as with other words that were used. One of the lovely ones, I remember, was when someone was talking about one of the chaps who was ill and he had been to see him. 'My God,' he said, 'he's one to an otomy!' Years after, thinking about it, it came to me. It dates back to the old times of Burke and Hare and body snatchers; you know they used to get bodies for anatomies, but in the end, the bodies and the skeletons were called anatomies, so if you were one for an otomy, you were one for a skeleton.

There were some other lovely words, anyone who was stupid was dommel and if you were perplexed you were mummered. The stump of a tree was 'mute' and a word that I still use and always thought was quite correct, but couldn't find in a dictionary anywhere, the case in which a nut fits was always the hud and in the autumn when they were ripening there were kids saying, 'Have you been up the nut tree, do them slip hud?' The green case was called the hud and I think it must be a corruption of hood, that's all I can think of.

You would find people in the time I'm talking about, saying some mornings, 'My God, that's gallos cold, aint it?' and then you'd hear them say,

'Aye, it's a gallos bad job.' Obviously with cold, as cold as the gallows, which is a pretty cold place, I should imagine, and afterwards through its use 'gallos cold', it's got the meaning of 'very', and so you could have a 'gallos bad job', and it seemed even in Scotland gallos was used for that sense.

There was an old lady, Dolly Franklin, who was the bothy woman. She saw to the bothy where the apprentice gardeners lived, and my mother said to her one day, 'Well, Mrs Franklin, you haven't got a watch, how do you know the time to cook the men's dinner?' and she replied, 'I always know because my inners womble.' Once the vegetable man in the garden had been out and had had a bit of a row with the cook at the big house and he said, ''Er look just flattened the snowing arbours.' Some time in the last century, there's been some bigwig etymologist who stated that the average rural worker had a vocabulary of about 500 words. That's absolute rubbish, they have a marvellous vocabulary. I expect they have 500 words connected to the horse and its harness.

There is a general feeling that the typical Englishman goes into under-statement. If something's really horrible, he says it's rather nasty, stiff upper lip business. Harold Macmillan, when there was a real crisis, called it 'a little local difficulty'. My recollection of talking with the typical working men of that time was just the opposite – they exaggerated like anything. It's what grammarians call hyperbole. I remember once it was a very mucky day and the track through the forest was a deep gully down Patch Riding from Finstock down to the kennels, and I said, 'I expect that was pretty messy down Patch Riding this morning, Ernie?' 'Messy,' he said, 'my God, that wasn't fit for a bird to fly across!' I came across just the same thing in Berkshire with the same type of individual. I had a neighbour, Fred Hand, who was the local blacksmith and I hadn't been there long when I wanted to scythe some grass. I couldn't get the scythe to go at all well, it wasn't set properly. I took it up to Fred's and asked him to get the scythe working properly for me. Fred ran his thumb along the blade and said, 'My God, I could ride bare assed to London on 'ee!'

In my boyhood, the lakes at Wychwood were deep and clean and well stocked with fish. The apparatus they used to cut the lake weeds was like the huge old hay knives linked together and put across the lake, so a team of men each side seesawed and walked right the way along and cut the weeds off right at the bottom. These unwanted weeds then floated down to the sluice and were gathered up and taken away, so you were left with lovely clean deep water. Now at this time, the particular lake I'm thinking of, called the Proud Lake, is nearly a solid mass of weeds, mainly mares-tail – which leads me to another thing, to do with words more than Wychwood.

I was going along this trout lake once and there were two men fishing. One of them said, 'My boy, would you mind going to the next gentleman and asking if I can have his lending net?' I quite thought a lending net was something you borrowed. So I went and asked this gentleman for his lending net. What I found afterwards was that the man who gave me sixpence for getting this lending net, was Sir Edward Grey, who later became Lord Grey of Falloden, who used to stay at Cornbury quite a lot, and of course what he'd wanted was a landing net!

One day we went out when the hunt came into the park and the forest. The fox happened to go by and old Jack gets up onto his legs and goes right down and gives a hooloo! Very shortly up gallops Captain Brassey from Heythrop, who was Master of the Hunt in those days. 'Did you see the fox, my man?' he asked Jack.

'Yes, sir,' Jack replied, looking mighty pleased with himself.

'Was it a tarred one?'

Jack looked puzzled for a moment, 'Tarred, Sir? Bugger never looked black however!' Another example of different pronunciation between one class and another … 'tired' and 'tarred'.

In Charlbury we used to have an Irish doctor, his father was Dr Crone, but because he was the son, he was always Dr 'Enery. Dr 'Enery was a great wag, always joking and pulling people's legs. One day a rather simple type of woman came in called Nell and as was the fashion in those days when winter was approaching, as she came up the steps he saw some red flannel showing and knew that she had her winter red flannel petticoats on. He sat Nell down in the chair and said, 'Open your mouth, please,' and she opened it. 'Say, aah!' She readily obliged. 'Oh, Nell,' he said, 'I see you've got your red flannel on already!' She just looked at him for a moment, but she was pretty quick and gently admonishing him, went one better. 'Ooh Doctor 'Enery, you be a one! Next thing you'll look up me arse to see if me hat's on straight!'

You have already discovered some of the poetry which Wychwood inspired Bill to write; here's a fairly early short story, which we found amongst his papers and clippings.

The Forest Folk
by Donald Campbell

'Hullo!' said a voice, 'Poaching again?' The Keeper poked his head over the bushes and grinned at me, as I sat crouched in the heather, whence I had been admiring a nimble, white-bellied weasel rippling in and out of the rabbit-tunnels in the gorse. Having cast off his cumbersome bag, which served him as game-bag, lunch-basket and ground sheet, the Keeper sat down beside me, his gun, as always, within reach.

'How are the birds?' I asked just to encourage him, for though he was on his way home after a long spell in the rearing-field, I knew that talking shop would start him off; keepering was his hobby as well as his work.

'Few more dead,' he grunted, as he filled his pipe with my tobacco, 'that new hand of ourn overfeeds 'em, then what's left is sour be next day, and poisons 'em. A jumped-up rabbit-catcher, that what he is, not a keeper.'

I murmured my complete agreement with his opinion, knowing better than to interrupt what looked like developing into a sound exposition of the whole art of rearing pheasants.

'Talking of rabbit-catchers,' he went on, 'I just see a danged Grey Squirrel a-chasing a sucker; they'll be tackling full-growed 'uns next, now as they've got the taste for rabbits. It's about time as – '

Here his voice, which had been growing more and more weary, gradually dwindled to complete silence, and I fancy he sprawled at ease on the heather, doubtless dreaming schemes for the complete extermination of his pet aversion. (It is always a nice point between us, that snooze; he always declares that he knows better than to go to sleep in company; but I must give my own account.)

Through the July haze the distant birches trembled in the heat, swarms of midgets danced their monotonous up-and-down dance, and a big silver-washed fritillary flitted dreamily from thistle to thistle, so I simply let my mind drift away with them; to have remained wide awake would have been an insult to Nature; I therefore chose the course which suited both her and myself.

Suddenly something quite close to me went 'Pop!' very solemnly and emphatically, and my weasel reappeared, and began a slow, ridiculous waltz, his forepaws upraised as if in prayer.

'Whatever's the matter?' I inquired, wondering vaguely if popping were a symptom of apoplexy, and if so, how could I get ice in this heat.

'We weasels always go 'Pop',' he answered surprisedly, 'it's quite traditional. 'Pop goes the weasel,' you know.' And he began to sing it, quickening his step to jig-time as he did so, for like all weasels he had a keen sense of rhythm. Nearer and nearer to me he danced, until his shrewd little face almost touched mine; then the singing ceased, and he confided in a whisper, 'We are having an indignation meeting.'

'Who are 'WE?' I asked; for he pronounced it as if it were spelled with large capitals.

He rolled his pale eyes, and said: 'Why, the Forest Folk, of course. The Jay-pie over there,' jerking his head toward a thorn where that brazen-voiced creature was screaming, 'is calling Feathered Folk. I, on account of my charm, or as the envious say, my hypnotic powers, am the Forest Crier for Furred Folk. A kind of Pied Piper, in fact,' he smirked, looking at his brown and white livery.

'How sharp you are,' I couldn't help remarking.

'Sharp as a weasel, in fact,' he retorted, and went on dancing, dancing.

A fat sleepy-looking rabbit peeped out from his hole, and stared as if he'd never seen the dance before. The bracken rustled, and slowly and slyly Toby loped along, his head almost on the ground, as if deep in thought. Behind him at a leisurely pace shambled Brock, and both lay under a large gorse-bush, for the sun was strong. Then came the Feathered Folk, the Pheasant walking warily past Toby, the Wren coming chirping through the under-growth to perch near the Sparrow-hawk. (I waited patiently for the lion and the lamb to frisk along, but in vain.)

Then all started talking together, until old Brock called for silence; they respected him, for he was a veteran, and naturally, as grey as a badger.

In his gruff rustic voice he began.

'Folk,' he said, 'this concerns both fur and feather, foxes and finches, flesh and fowl. 'Tis these foreign varmin as have come to the Forest. First there's this Grey Squirrel. Strangers we can put up wi', in season; but when they settle and breed as fast as flies, and pretty nigh do away wi' them as have been here as long as the Forest,' here he cast a sympathetic eye on the last Red Squirrel, 'then 'tis time as we did summat.'

'I'll tear him to shreds,' yapped Toby.

'I'll bore two neat holes in his grey neck, and do the job neatly,' said the weasel, his eyes aflame, so that the rabbit trembled..

Brock continued: 'What's more, they ain't got no manners. Dance about in trees and swear at honest folk in some heathen tongue, they do.'

'Choctaw, I imagine,' said the White Owl, poking her ghostly heart-shaped. face from a hollow in the oak above; and, since she was as wise as an owl, none gainsayed her.

'Only this morning,' Brock rumbled on, 'Old Jason remarked to Levi, as they came down Five Ash Bottom, "These 'ere greyified rat-squirrels be'aved as pleasant as snow in 'arvest."'

In the angry puttering which followed, the White Owl shrilled her complaint. 'What about this insolent Little Owl that's come to the Forest too?' she hooted. 'He's a foreigner and a disgrace to our name. Flies by day, and cuts clumsy antics, same as I've heard tell the clowns at Forest Fair used to.'

'He reckons to be a bit antic-weighted too,' said the Weasel. His diet, I think, made him so full of animal spirits. 'Says his likeness was stamped on silver in Ancient Greece, where he was much looked up to.'

'Look up, look up, look up, look up!' crowed the Pheasant, taking up the Weasel's last words. The Hawk sat and stared, and knowing he had eyes like a hawk, Toby and Brock followed his gaze, and with muzzles twitching, agreed that there was something in the wind.

Suddenly ears, eyes and noses of the whole assembly came to the same decision, and a great shout went up. 'A Grey 'un – after him!'

'Now,' screamed the Weasel to the Hawk, 'drive him to ground, and Weasel, catch him.'

'Is this the time to pun?' grumbled Brock, rushing to guard the foot of the maple in whose crown the grey 'un perched.

'That's not a pun,' retorted the Weasel pertly, 'it's our traditional half-a-pun. You know – 'Half a pun of tuppenny rice –' and off he went into his ridiculous chorus, until he attempted a particularly loud 'Pop'; I knew it would happen if he persisted: he went off with a terrific blast that quite dispersed the meeting.

I opened my eyes to see the smoke wreathing around the Keeper's gun-muzzle. 'I'll teach you to swear at your betters, you rat-faced furriner,' he was saying to a grey carcase.

8

FUNGI AND FLOWERS

A part from his numerous radio programmes, Bill's spoken words can still be heard in the several Sounds Natural cassettes to which he was the major contributor. There are five titles in all, some of which have already featured in different parts of the book, but now there is a chance to share in his natural history wisdom, starting with some excerpts from *A Fungus Foray*, recorded in 1981 in a coniferous part of Wychwood. As in most of the other titles, his companion on the other side of the microphone was Ken Jackson. As they began their autumn walk, Ken wondered why you cannot go on a fungus foray at other times of the year.

Because most of the year, most of the plant is invisible. What we usually regard as fungi are really corresponding organs to flowers and fruits in green plants. Most of the year, and often for many years, the actual plant, which is roughly a mass of cobwebby threads, is feeding and growing on some organic tissue, either alive or dead, often wood, often soil. Then, usually in the autumn, but not invariably in some species, up comes its reproductive organs, the spore-bearing parts, mushrooms and toadstools and puff-balls and things like that, and I imagine that the majority of them fruit in autumn, because then the soil is at its warmest – it isn't in midsummer – it takes a long time for the soil to heat up and a long time to cool down. I think it's a combination of that – autumn is usually damp and the ground's fairly warm and that's the time when they sprout. The spores are not equivalent to the seeds of flowers, because they are single celled – just one cell, whereas a seed may be made up of thousands of cells. It is a bit tricky to be dogmatic about this, but there is one school of naturalists now who regard fungi as neither plants nor animals, but a distinct kingdom, because they are so different in so many ways. Although most of the names are Latin, they have English names, usually if they're known to be edible, or if they're known to be poisonous, so you get death cap, destroying angel, the fly agaric, which is pretty but poisonous, and then you get all sorts of others which are edible, like the penny bun, and the shaggy cap or the lawyer's wig, ink cap. But there again that's a very good example, because the shaggy ink cap, which comes up like a blunt steeple-shaped thing and is very, very scaly – white – is totally edible and in my opinion better than mushrooms, more delicate. When it gets older, it doesn't drop its spores in the form of powder, it liquifies, deliquesces and black inky stuff comes out. Now, there's another one very much like it, except it isn't scaly, and isn't so elongated in its early state, but it's also a *Coprinus*, it tastes equally good, but if you take a glass of wine or a glass of beer with a meal when you eat it, it makes you horribly ill and so that's a good example of how careful you ought to be. There are others that are perfectly good to eat cooked and are poisonous raw, because some people do eat fungi raw.

In some of the more minute types, one with which I'm sure gardeners will be very familiar – and I can see a bit on a twig over there – if you've used sticks for supporting plants, say pea-sticks or supporting herbaceous plants or any thing like that, you'll find they're useless next year, because they've gone brittle and dead and the chief cause of it is this, you see it's rather a pretty colour, isn't it? Aptly it's called coral spot fungus and I think it's about the commonest one which destroys young twigs once they're severed from a plant; you see it universally. The next commonest one I know is rather larger and browner, and it's very common on the dead bark of beech trees. Here's one on a piece of dead wood that grows up like a miniature stag-horn. There's a whole group of these, one called the candlewick fungus and there are several others thicker and rightly, I think, you can call them club fungi. There are one or two fungi that are specific to certain types of plants, for instance there's a white bracket fungus that grows on birch and nothing else and there's another bracket that looks just like a burnt bun and I think its favourite is ash, I haven't seen it on anything else, sometimes called King Alfred's cakes, for obvious reasons. The ear fungus is nearly always only found on elder, though there are exceptions. Here's another amongst the leaves at our feet, that's been eaten by something … . Ah, it's a blewit, Ken! isn't it beautiful? A mauvy blue and not only humans fancy it, I should say squirrel – you can see the toothmarks. Pity there aren't more, because that's a lovely one to eat.

Ah, ha! Now this is one I've been looking for, this is a bracket and it grows in concentric rings, different colours, this is a very old one, but the outer one always has a white rim – *coriolis versicolor* (turning colour). You notice if you look underneath, you can see the little holes, the tubes, that's the spore bearing part. I think this is one of the perennials – some of the bracket fungi are – but you see there's a dead layer like wood, then another one and another one and then this current one which is white. I've known this one in my time used for sharpening the old cut-throat razors, they're so beautifully smooth and firm.

You notice, Ken, as we were coming up here, I was sniffing, because I knew that somewhere in this area there's one of the most interesting and in some ways the most loathsome of them all. That, as you can guess, is the stinkhorn. Let's get the right side of the wind! Now this is interesting, you'd think it was a pigeon's egg coming up through the ground, a pure white little dome. Then, it pushes up very rapidly and breaks open. You can see the remains of the ball at the bottom, you see, and up comes this stem, then it has that cap with a spongy texture, which oozes slimy liquid which stinks exactly like decaying carrion. The dripping stuff coming off the cap is swarming with its spores, flies come to it. They drink what they think is rotten meat presumably and the spores, which are indigestible, pass through them and so are transferred to another site. The other day when I came here, you couldn't see those caps, it looked like a small swarm of bees on it. Usually, it's either bluebottles or greenbottles, but I'm sure this is a robber fly and it was covered with those the other day – it's a long brownish fly and normally they attack and suck the juice of insects. It's years and years since I found stinkhorn and this year it's everywhere. The funny thing is I found it in the main forest the other day and it was very evocative. My first-ever was found there when we were searching – we'd been asked by the keeper to keep an eye open for the corpse of a deer that he was sure he'd killed. Dusk was coming on when he'd been looking and he said let me know if you find it. Three or four days later, we both sniffed and said, 'Dead deer!' We went into this hollow and found our first stinkhorns ever. This year, I found it in exactly the same place and, by a great coincidence, a rutting buck in the wood just behind me was groaning at the same time, so it connected up with the deer of the past.

The following are excerpts from a tape entitled *Wild Flowers and Country Cures*. Bill and Ken were walking again in the ancient forest of Wychwood, in June this time, when they came across deadly nightshade.

Yes, this is the real genuine deadly nightshade. Now I say that because I think ninety-nine people out of a hundred call this other one, which is luckily growing within sight, this one with the brilliant little scarlet berries growing in a cluster and little purplish mauve flowers with a yellow centre, very much like a miniature potato flower, they call this, deadly nightshade, but this is woody nightshade or bitter-sweet and a comparatively harmless plant. It grows straggly and is almost a climber.

Now why I think this is such a pity, is that if the general populace think this is deadly nightshade and teach their children so, they won't know the real and truly deadly thing when they see it. It's nothing like the common woody nightshade, to start with, it's a huge robust clump and its flower is a brownish purple bell, nearly the size of a thimble and it looks sullen and sinister to me. But this is the important thing at this time of the year, these beautiful berries certainly look enticing, succulent, brilliant, glossy jet black, almost as big as cherries, slightly flatter, beautifully set in five star-shape sepals. Now three of these have proved to be a fatal dose for children, who quite naturally think they're edible, because they certainly look it, don't they? They are edible for those creatures for whom they are intended, the only two I know of with any certainty, are pheasants and blackbirds.

But you'll also see, Ken, the leaves of this are riddled by, in this case, slugs, but sometimes there're eaten by more minute insects and obviously with impunity, but to humans they are lethal. The foliage is not unlike a potato's, they are the same family, Solanaceae, of course a great number of that family are poisonous, although potato and tomato are quite useful. It has quite an interesting history; I think the name is triply warning – you've got the nightshade, both suggesting darkness and then you've got deadly as well, so I mean the name's enough. It was used in medicine from early times, but the trouble was of course with all the old herbal treatments, the matter of standardising doses. In the end, one of the old herbalists such as the sixteenth-century famous one, John Gerrard, said, 'My council is to banish this plant from your gardens and the use thereof, because it is so furious and deadly.'

It was only when more sophisticated methods became available to apothecaries in the nineteenth century that it was discovered that the extract purified and placed in the human eye caused the pupil to dilate tremendously so that the oculist could examine the state of the eye, and it still is the basis in drops for an eye examination. Apart from that, I don't think it's used much, although there are hundreds of compounds of this poison, atropine. The Italian name for it is belladonna, beautiful lady, because an extract from it, I think it was the distillation from it, was used by ladies to enlarge the pupils of their eyes and make them look more beautiful.

Now, here is a plant called henbane. Any plants called bane were supposed to be poisonous to the creature involved. There's fleabane and leopard's bane, 'though heaven knows how often people wanted to kill leopards in England! I don't think it kills hens or ever did, but it's a poisonous plant and it does grow on disturbed ground and as a matter of fact, the biggest colony I've ever seen, there were scores of them, was on a field that had been scratched by hens, so perhaps because it came up in hen runs, it was called henbane. The interesting thing is that although it doesn't look anything like deadly nightshade, it is a relative, a member of the same family. I think it is a more beautiful flower, pale, yellowish- creamy, veined with faint purple and then a deep purple centre. There is still something sinister about it and if you smell it, it's really horrible, it smells poisonous and that's that. I think it's more common in East Anglia on some of the dry and often bare sandy fields, where you can see quite a lot of it; it can make magnificent plants and grow to four or five feet tall. It's a good example of what the old herbalists used to call the 'doctrine of signatures'. That is, they thought that the Almighty had placed in plants various clues telling what they were good for. For instance, woundwort and herb Robert, both very reddish plants, were good for healing wounds, you see the connection with blood and the red.

Now this is toothwort and there are two theories here, either because of this toothed calyx, or because when it goes to seed, like this one with a whole cluster of seeds like teeth in a jaw, obviously they thought, that's a sign, so extracts of this were used for toothache. I think it certainly would be efficacious, for it contains almost the identical drug of deadly nightshade, atropine, but this is hyoscyamine and it has a numbing effect upon nerves and muscles and so it probably would cure the toothache, but probably finish the patient off as well! Now this still persists in medicine, extracts from it, very highly prepared, for a brain sedative; it was used in preparations before the main anaesthetic for an operation and used to be used in cases of madness, all because it has this sedative effect upon the brain. It also stops chronic hiccups and things like that, because it has a paralysing effect on the muscles. Now the last development, with the increase in travel by sea and air, is that it's been found this same compound, hyoscyamine and derivatives thereof, has a paralysing effect upon the stomach muscles and therefore prevents seasickness. Lots of these standard ones, I mustn't use any names here, do have hyoscyamine in them. Not just the berries were used in this way, but a decoction of all the parts of the plant, but I think they used to use a decoction made from the seeds for toothache.

This is the true wild aquilegia, the columbine, nearly always blue, but very occasionally you get a pink one. This is one of the places I've known it for years and years. Here there is a narrow ride only six or seven yards wide, tall trees on either side, but as we're standing now in glorious early morning dappled sunshine, we can see over 100 clumps along this edge here in full bloom. They look so cool in this light. You know, Ken, even if it had no flowers it would be a beautiful plant, because of its lovely foliage. A beautiful pale green, trefoil, each individual leaflet trefoil again, and then these very dainty flowers. Near the flowers are bracts, which are single leaves. Peculiar plant, you wouldn't think it was a relation of the buttercup, but it is.

The name columbine is interesting, because it means dove-like. At first sight there's nothing to suggest a little dove, but you have to look at it from above, because it hangs upside down. You see, those five hook parts, the spurs, are the nectaries, and the insects' long tongues have to poke all the way down. But to ancient people, they suggested five birds in a nest sitting up, you see that? Five clustered pigeons, or doves, but it shows what poor ornithologists they were, because pigeons and doves only have two young, blackbirds or thrushes or robins would have been much better, but that's the origin of the name. I don't think it's ever been used medicinally, but here again in one of those absurd old myths, which were all on the go in medieval times, it was reputed that lions ate this to give them courage, I don't know where they found it in lion country, in lion habitat, but because of that, it was a practice to rub one's hands with this before a fight or battle, to get the courage the lions got!

The cultivated columbine is not I think as attractive as the wild one. There are a number of hybrids with North American ones, which have red and yellow colours in them and there are some nice little Alpine ones, miniatures of these. Incidentally, it has a terrific lot of nicknames, particularly in the west country. I think it's in hedges in Devon and Somerset and so on, where it's most abundant. In Dorset, as children we always used to know this as 'granny's bonnet', and it's 'grandmother's bonnet, widows' weeds', because its shape is something like the bonnets old folk used to wear. It's the month of June and already wild arum, or lords and ladies, are over. The sheaf is withering and the seeds, like a bunch of green grapes, will be the red berries of autumn when the leaves have pretty well died down. It has a fascinating pollination story, which involves the trapping of insects. There's a valve, like a green hood sticking up, you see, it wraps round into a valve and beneath it in a sort of container, are the essential reproductive parts, and it has the spikes sticking up and it has a strong smell which attracts little midges. They go in, pass the hairs pointing downwards, one-way traffic, and get trapped in the receptacle below and are just kept there, until the pollen ripens and just falls on them. As soon as that happens, the hairs wither and the insects go out and into another wild arum and so the pollen gets transferred from one plant to another. It is I think one of the most interesting stories amongst British plants. Both this plant and even more so, the one that occurs in the south of England, so-called 'Italian wild arum', have an interesting history. During the Napoleonic wars, arrowroot was apparently a very favourite food, particularly for invalids and a lot was imported, but with Napoleon's blockade, it became short. Someone offered what in those days was called a premium, a prize for anyone who could produce a substitute for arrowroot that could be grown in Britain. Particularly on the Isle of Portland, they made this floury stuff from the roots of arum; it was called 'Portland Arrowroot' and it was very successful apparently, quite nutritious. The root had to be ground up, soaked to get the poison out and the starchy remnant made into flour. The berries are a very good source of food for blackbirds and warblers which stay here late, like blackcaps.

Now, here is silverweed, a plant with a yellow flower like a buttercup until you look at its leaves, which are like silver feathers, or ferns. They are covered in numerous minute hairs, which give it that effect. It is growing in the middle of this hard trodden path, but it doesn't upset it at all. Silverweed had several properties, again for healing wounds mainly, but it was thought it must be good for one's feet since it grew in such places, feet were good for it, so it was good for feet! Always a plant of trodden places, it seems to thrive on it. It was recommended for carriers, to put in their boots to stop their feet from getting too hot when they had long walks to do and that was actually done; might be worth trying on a hot day like this, but I dare say dandelion leaves would do as well!

This plant is one of the most interesting in the forest and not in flower until the autumn. Its properties are well known and it's one of the few still in use and approved medicinally. It's not a crocus, although it's like a crocus, but belongs to a different group with a slightly different number of parts. It's a *Colchicum*, called the 'autumn crocus' and also 'meadow saffron', but since saffron is a crocus it still isn't correct. It has a lot of lovely nicknames and I think the commonest one is 'naked lady', because about the end of August and beginning of September, this area will be a mass of just flowers without any trace of foliage, not even a green stem; it's only the flower above ground, about 6 to 9 inches high, of a beautiful pinky mauve and there will be sheets of them down here, as you can see by the huge amount of their foliage. The plant in flower is then completely dormant, there's not a leaf to be seen. Only part of the flower is above ground, and it has a very long tube from the petals going down to the ovary above the bulb. Then in the following spring, up come the leaves, as you see, great big rushy ones. Here, just emerging is a great fat capsule, the ovary, which is the result of last year's autumn crocus. It's the seed box which comes above ground in the spring and that is how it reproduces. Of course the ordinary spring crocus does that, you know, except they have foliage when they flower; you'll notice the ovary in those is just below the surface and comes up in the spring on a stem. *Colchicum* is very poisonous, by the way, and its great quality is in the cure for gout, or at least an alleviation for gout, and it is still used for that purpose. In the old days, two counties in particular, Oxfordshire and Gloucestershire, used to send terrific amounts of these to London hospitals, until the beginning of the 18th century. I think that's why you only see them growing in masses like this in private grounds, because the rest, almost entirely, had been gathered and dug up and sent away to make a few pence, and also probably they were done away with for being poisonous to cattle. Here in a private woodland, there is a reserve for it where it was never exploited in that way.

Jo Dunn was a near neighbour of Bill's in Charlbury who shared his interest and enthusiasm for plants, especially wild flowers. She had consulted him on the subject of birds some twenty years earlier but, as she wrote when, knowing her botanical skills, we asked her for a contribution to this chapter:

It was more recently, after learning that Bill was also keenly interested in wild flowers, that I became better acquainted with him. One summer he took me to see a large cluster of the tall milky bellflower (*Campanula lactiflora*) growing near the estate sawmill at Cornbury. Although not a native plant but a long-established garden escape, it was a most impressive and beautiful sight.

Preoccupied for several years after that with my own botanical interests and activities, it was not until the early summer of 1991 that we met again to talk about plants. He had just been driven to the north of England by one of his former pupils to see the very rare lady's slipper orchid, only one or two of which have survived the predations of unscrupulous collectors. Strictly guarded by day and night by plant conservationists, no one was allowed near the site, but Bill and his companion, from a viewpoint some distance away, were thrilled to catch a glimpse of this lovely orchid through their binoculars. That story led us to talk about wild orchids and to recall the different species we had seen and the places where they grew. It was perhaps the same good friend who had taken him to see the bog orchid in Hampshire. As I had never seen this rarity, he very kindly took a piece of paper and drew a sketch map to show me how to find it, adding that before leaving the site he had marked one little group of plants with a dead stick. It was not until six years later that I was able to visit the New Forest with a botanist friend. We took Bill's sketch map with us, and without too much difficulty found the site and eventually a group of four little plants marked by a stick. Whether this was Bill's original stick or one that had later replaced it, or whether this was a different set of plants, it was impossible to say, but we were delighted to find the orchids and photograph them.

A visit to Bill usually ended with an invitation to accompany him on a walk around his garden. He grew flowers, both cultivated and wild, shrubs (many chosen to attract butterflies or to provide berries for birds in winter), vegetables and soft fruit. There were also a few fruit trees. Being a naturalist's garden there was plenty of wildlife interest too. Early in the spring there were violets and the double-flowered celandines given to him by Ken and Mary Jackson who had inherited them in their garden. In summer one border contained tall native teasels, grown to provide seeds for goldfinches. He also had a few plants of the alien cut-leaved teasel, raised from seed gathered from plants he had found in a gravel pit at Stanton Harcourt. Descendents of these can be seen on the bank opposite the platform at Charlbury railway station. It is thought that these plants possibly originated from seed carried there by goldfinches.

Less than a year after his motoring accident in the summer of 1991, though often short of breath, he expressed a wish to see the wild columbines in Wychwood. So one afternoon in May I drove him over towards Leafield and accompanied him into the forest. He knew exactly where to look and during the time we spent there we counted about two hundred plants. I was frequently nervous on his behalf, but, as I had observed before, once a goal was set, nothing deterred him. If beds of stinging nettles, overhanging trees, bushes or wire threatened to impede him he would, with his stick, find a way through.

He was in his eighty-ninth year when I happened to mention that in a few days time I would be meeting a small party of botanists monitoring the rare Cotswold penny-cress at a site about four miles away. He knew the plant well, and had written about it in one of his Country Diaries and was keen to see it again. So I offered to take him with me. He was very pleased to see the plants, and also to meet a few people he knew; and two strangers

Phyllis Mond taking Bill Campbell in a wheelchair to see the Meadow Saffron in Wychwood in
September 1994.

who were regular readers of his Country Diary were delighted to be introduced to him.

One of Bill's last wishes was to see the meadow saffron in Wychwood. Sometimes called the autumn crocus, it is in fact a member of the lily family, flowering in late summer and early autumn. This wish was fulfilled in September 1994 through the kindness of his good friends Peter and Phyllis Mond, who took him there in a wheelchair. This farewell visit to the forest he had known and loved since boyhood affected him deeply.

9

GUARDIAN COUNTRY DIARIES AND SOME OTHER WRITINGS

For many years Bill wrote a weekly Country Diary for *The Guardian*, a good selection of which you'll find reproduced in four of the following chapters. We're grateful to *The Guardian* for permission to let you read them here. He began writing them in 1964, sharing with readers his vast knowledge of bird life, natural history and gardening. His visits to the Isles of Scilly and Portland Bill gave readers annual updates on the passage of bird life.

Jeannette Page, the writer of the Foreword to this book, was in charge of A Country Diary and as she wrote in the *Guardian* the day after he died,

> His garden became the readers' garden, his village their village and his sorrow at the passing of country life their sorrow. He was outspoken in his criticism of the bureaucratic pen which, for example, had made his Berkshire Downs haunts part of Oxfordshire. And when Oxford was removed from his address, he spared no quarter in his attack on the Post Office. 'The powers-that-be have failed to realise that, apart from the prestige of Oxford in the address, the new postal centre is cut off nearly every year whenever snowdrifts block the road.'

In 1994 Jeanette Page edited a *Guardian* book entitled *A Country Diary*, which is a collection of diary entries covering a period of almost 30 years – the same time that WD was one of the diarists.

As well as writing for *The Guardian* for all these years, Bill contributed regularly to *The Countryman* magazine. Here's a piece from spring 1948 – long before he started his Country Diaries:

Food for Birds and Man
by W. D. Campbell

The bird enthusiast who claims that all birds do good all the time rightly infuriates any observant gardener or farmer. On the other hand, the economic ornithologist is equally exasperated by the person who, having had peas stripped by dawn patrols of jays and hawfinches, brassica seedlings and crocus blooms ruined by house-sparrows, forsythia and pear blossoms nipped in the bud by bullfinches, or a cherry crop ravaged by starlings and blackbirds, sees only the other side of the picture.

For those who know only the evidence for the prosecution, I suggest a visit to an oak wood in bluebell time, when the minute voidings of the tortrix moth larvae make a miniature but plainly audible hail as they fall without ceasing on the dog's mercury below. These caterpillars form one of the chief foods for rearing nestlings at this season, and such potential pests as jays, jackdaws, great tits, house-sparrows, chaffinches, starlings and blackbirds are all among the food-gatherers. Yet, in spite of such natural control, oaks are sometimes defoliated.

Last year the gardener part of me noted with some annoyance that one visit from a family of great tits had ruined a score or so of my best pea-pods, but the ornithologist part knew something of the family history of this brood. As far as I could gather from many hours' watching, the sole food of the young during their last week in the nest was obtained from my neighbour's Newton Wonder and the nearby blacksmith's Ribston Pippin, both of which were badly attacked by caterpillars. Two sample counts of an hour's duration, each undertaken on different days, showed that a beakful of grubs (dripping over in a manner reminiscent of a puffin laden with sprats) was taken to the nest every minute, each parent keeping to one tree. The fact that my excellent unnamed cooker was unvisited, although badly infested with caterpillar, stresses the importance of cultivating an altruistic approach to this problem.

Some years ago I ringed some hundreds of blackbirds in their winter roosts a few miles from Burford; of these many were recovered in the same locality throughout the year; others moved south and west, one was recovered on the Hampshire coast and another near Holyhead. A third bird was recovered on her nest on the Danish island of Fynen during the following May. Thus the blackbirds enlivening the dusk as they go shrilly to roost may be the culprits who reduced your fruit yield, they may be innocent British moorland birds whose dessert consisted of blackberries and rowan berries farther north, or again they may be Continental aliens.

The feeding habits of the starling have aroused almost as much controversy as those of the little owl, and since this species is so plentiful and gregarious, its economic status is of some importance. Our native summer flocks can undoubtedly be a plague in plum and cherry districts and in droughty weather show a discriminating taste in apples and pears. But even in summer starlings do a great deal to control the cranefly pest, both by their peculiar open-beaked probing for leather jackets in turf, and by a rather gauche imitation of the swallow in taking daddy-long-legs on the wing. The huge winter flocks, the internationalists, are almost entirely beneficial. A few years ago gamekeepers tried to stop a 'murmuration of stares' roosting in certain shrubberies and thickets. I used to visit the scene and gather corpses, removing the gizzards for later analysis. During December, January and February I examined the food of eighty starlings in this way, and found that the average content of one bird was seven wireworms, six small beetles (including the click-beetle, the adult stage of the wireworm), eleven leather-jackets, thirteen small snails and three corn grains. These figures probably represent a minimum, not a true total, since some of the food consumed in the early morning would have passed beyond the gizzard by nightfall. Almost ten million starlings have been estimated to breed in this country and this figure is increased several-fold by winter immigration; if this vast number consumes anything like my sample on some hundred and fifty days of the year, the species plays no little part in food production. Even with this potent control force, much of our newly-broken arable land is wireworm-infested.

This difference between the numbers and habits of residents during the breeding season, and those of the cosmopolitan flocks in winter, is also seen in the wood-pigeon. Even though this bird is almost entirely a pest, small summer parties will often do a certain amount of scavenging on fallows, and I have opened crops which bulged with dock and charlock seed. The smaller stock-dove is even better for this purpose. Once beech-masts and acorns have been consumed, however, the large winter flocks of pigeons concentrate almost entirely on greenstuff and clover.

If we concede that the wood-pigeon is almost a complete pest, we thereby partially absolve the jay from the same charge, for it is a great consumer of the pigeons' conspicuous eggs. I have even witnessed the unpleasant spectacle of half-grown pigeon squabs being eaten by a jay. To curse the wood-pigeons which drop in some summer morning and skeletonise your newly set-out brussel sprouts, and then to shoot the jay which desires some fruit to round off a meal of those same visitors' eggs, is typical of our inconsistent approach to such problems. The use of efficient fire-arms, for almost two centuries, to keep down the numbers of such natural pigeon predators as peregrines, harriers, sparrow-hawks, magpies and jays, has led in its turn to the expenditure of further powder and shot in pigeon shoots.

Fruit growers may be consoled by the knowledge that blackbirds' nests are also robbed by jays; but so are those of the far more useful song-thrush. In fact, a clutch of the thrush's eggs by an open gin is a favourite device of a certain type of game-keeper. To be fair, however, it must be admitted that this lack of discrimination is not peculiar to the jay – the useful spotted flycatcher snaps up a bee or an ichneumon fly as readily as it does a cabbage-white or a daddy-long-legs.

The gardener's favourite bird is not always the most useful one. The robin and the song-thrush probably head the poll, yet I continually catch both of these favourites in traps baited with soft fruit for warblers and nightingales. The only blameless birds, from a gardener's point of view, are the one-hundred per cent insect-eaters, all of necessity summer visitors – for example, swallows, flycatchers, swifts and nightjars. Even then, one-hundred per cent insect food is not necessarily one-hundred per cent pest consumption. Apart from the lapwing, that most useful of all birds to the arable farmer (and even to the sheep farmer, by its consumption of fluke-carrying snails), I can think only of the wren, hedge-sparrow, and marsh and long-tailed tits as common residents which are useful at all seasons.

The mouse-like treecreeper, unobtrusively searching every crack and cranny on a fruit tree from bole to twig-tip, is a specialist feeder, equipped with supple curved beak and woodpecker-like stance for one purpose only – tree cleaning. If only this species were as plentiful as the house-sparrow, grease-bands and tar-oils could be dispensed with.

The tits being both gregarious and vocal, are more sure of notice than treecreepers, and likewise do a deal to clean up dormant fruit trees, although they are less thorough workers. Repeated visits, however, do much to atone for slipshod workmanship.

The wren performs a useful task in exploring a stratum of the garden neglected by most other birds, except perhaps the hedge-sparrow – the area immediately above the ground, such as the bottom of a hedge or herbaceous clump, or beneath the foliage of greenstuff and potatoes; no corner seems too dark or tangled for its bustling explorations. Next to the warblers, it is the species which I most frequently catch with aphides, and the only one trapped with egg-clusters of the cabbage-white butterfly as bait. I must admit that I have caught Jenny in a trap baited with red currants, but since no berry was punctured and since I repeatedly catch her in unbaited traps, I conclude that insatiable curiosity rather than a fruit diet explains her presence.

Of the summer migrants, the true insect-eaters are far outnumbered by the less spectacular group of warblers. Of these the whitethroat, willow warbler and chiffchaff are the commonest species. Rambler roses, honeysuckle, sweet and green peas and runner beans are favourite hunting grounds, when they visit gardens. On a single day in July I have ringed as many as twenty of these birds on one row of peas only twelve yards long, using as bait a broad-bean leaf black with fly. It should be noted that these aphides were not the original attraction – traps were set only when warblers were seen to be frequenting the site, possibly in search of thrips. Two years ago I ringed over eighty warblers from one sallow bush and a few bramble clumps at the edge of a field of Majestic potatoes, then in full bloom. As this situation had not been so productive of birds in previous seasons when it was under cereal crops, I walked through the baulks to see if the attraction lay in the potatoes, and in quite a small area flushed about twenty warblers, a pair each of nightingales and song-thrushes, and one hedge sparrow. Of the two possible food-sources, one was the small peach aphis, which is the vector of many virus diseases of potatoes; the other was a neutral insect, a minute black beetle which abounded on the blossoms. It is to be found on many flowers unvisited by bees, and I have used it successfully, in the cups of evening primroses, to catch warblers. As it will not 'stay put' as well as the more sluggish aphis, I use it only when short of bait. Caterpillars, which are appreciated as food by the larger whitethroat, also need constant replacement. The pale green larva of the small white butterfly, whose protective colouring and skulking habit by day suggest its palatability, is the best I have used; that of the nearly-related large white, flaunting its warning colours as it feeds in full daylight, is of course useless.

In spite of such excellent feeding habits, warblers cannot be included in the list of entirely blameless birds, as they are just as readily caught on raspberries and red currants. But one such fruit would fill so tiny a stomach, whereas the same space packed with aphides, thrips and insect ova would represent the salvation of an infinitely greater amount of produce. Other warblers, such as the blackcap, lesser whitethroat and garden-warbler, are more attracted to fruit than to insects. The lesser whitethroat is particularly fond of a really ripe greengage, but on using these as bait I discovered that a fruit already started on by blackbirds, starlings or wasps was necessary. On the few occasions when I have trapped nightingales, fruit has always been the bait.

Owls, of course, need no publicity as friends of plant growers, but no harm will be done by reinforcing their already secure position by a few facts. One hundred and ninety-three pellets of one barn-owl, which a group of my pupils are observing, have on analysis yielded remains of 370 mice and voles, 47 rats, 137 shrews, 16 beetles and 6 birds. The shrews, being largely carnivorous, may be regarded as an economic loss; the birds were two starlings, two house-sparrows, a chaffinch and a hedge-sparrow. But the preponderance of harmful rodents consumed far outweighs any loss of neutral or partly beneficial life. Dahlia growers may be pleased to know that the much maligned little owl, in addition to mice and beetles, is very partial to earwigs during the summer – the horny pincers being the only evidence left in the pellet.

The occurrence of certain species of birds in a garden may be governed by several outside factors. If woodland is at any distance jays and hawfinches are not likely to visit without the aid of intervening trees or bushes as stepping-stones, for they dislike long cross-country flights. The presence of hollow trees, quarries or disused chimneys in the vicinity will encourage jackdaws. Nearness to houses and farm buildings will mean house-sparrows, but as a compensation may encourage swallows, martins, swifts, and barn-owls. Gamekeepers in the neighbourhood may mean more summer pigeons through destruction of magpies, jays, kestrels and owls – protected owls as well as little owls.

The basic fact which must be grasped before this whole subject can be viewed sensibly is that gardening and farming are artificial. Consider a bramble hedge in full fruit, with one whitethroat feeding at random among the thousands of berries. In spite of the apparently long odds against such a chance, I can catch that bird in a trap baited with blackberries, the only difference being that my bunch is made up of specially selected berries, rendered even more conspicuous by the use of very pale foliage, such as a reversed raspberry leaf, as a plate. In the same way our unnatural massing of plants of superior succulence, and the further exposure of them by spacing, weeding or pruning, makes both them and their attendant pests the obvious target for birds which would otherwise forage for wild fruits.

W. D. Campbell, who is now at a school in Berkshire, tells us that he has been collecting the facts here presented 'during 30 years of gardening, 20 years of teaching of rural subjects, and 15 years of bird-catching'.

Country Life readers also benefited from WD's writing – indeed in 1965 Country Life Publications published *Birds of Town and Village*, with text by Bill, paintings by Basil Ede, and a foreword by H.R.H. The Prince Philip, Duke of Edinburgh. In July 1963 this appeared in the magazine:

A British Humming Bird
by W. D. Campbell

A few years ago ornithologists manning the bird observatory on Portland Bill were puzzled by the presence of some unidentified substance adhering to the bills and facial feathers of newly arrived spring migrants. Pollen, with some cementing material, was suspected, and accordingly samples from two whitethroats and one blackcap were sent to Kew for analysis. In all three cases pollen of some citrus species was found – that of orange alone on one whitethroat, with traces of another species, possibly lemon, on the other two birds. This in itself was not much of a clue as to the route by which these immigrants had entered Europe, since citrus fruits are cultivated around the whole Mediterranean.

As a result of this initial discovery British ornithologists intensified their researches in subsequent springs, not only at southern British points of entry but also (and most successfully of all numerically) in the Camargue in southern France. From these investigations it became clear that flowers were an important source of food for warblers on spring passage. Blackcaps were apparently the most habitual flower visitors – no less than 8 per cent of some 300 examined carried proof of this: chiffchaffs came next with 4 per cent. Although citrus pollen predominated, other clues as to plants visited were provided by both pollen and resin of some species of pine, pollens of sycamore and a liliaceous plant, probably an aloe, and, most plentiful of all on British-caught chiffchaffs, the pollen of bog-myrtle The latter was of special interest and significance, because two different species, *Myrica gale* and *M. faya*, were indicated. The former of these is our native bog-myrtle or sweet gale, which occurs in Western Europe from Spain northwards: but the second species is indigenous to the Azores, Madeira and the Canaries. It thus seems highly probable that chiffchaffs carrying pollen of this exotic species had wintered in those islands.

Since none of the birds concerned had been observed in the act of visiting flowers, one can only deduce the probable nature of the food sought at these sources. Blackcaps have been seen to tear open the flowers of hibiscus and aloe in order to drink the otherwise inaccessible nectar and they would be able to sip from the shallower orange-blossom without any preliminary violence. Many warblers visit flowers in order to seek insects, and it is usually assumed that newly-arrived willow warblers and chiffchaffs are attracted to sallows on this account. Since the 'pussy-willow' catkins on these trees produce nectar as well as pollen, pollination by insects is the normal procedure; their attractiveness to insectivorous birds is therefore understandable, particularly at a season when few such sources are available. But the bog-myrtle, having no such device for attracting insects, relies solely on the wind as its pollen-carrier: its male catkins may attract the occasional pollen-seeker, but there is no evidence for this supposition. Since the chiffchaffs had obviously been in direct contact with the male catkins, it is possible that the anthers themselves were being eaten – both siskins and great tits have been observed feeding in this manner on the catkins of aspen.

All this evidence leads to another revolutionary conclusion: that some European birds may act as pollinators of flowers just as effectively as the humming-birds of the New World or the sunbirds of the Old World tropics. The blackcap ranging the orange-groves could hardly avoid transferring pollen from one flower to another, but the chiffchaff would perform no such involuntary service for the bog-myrtle, since there is nothing to attract it to the separate female flowers.

But last summer in my Berkshire garden a chiffchaff demonstrated to me that it could behave as a humming-bird, both in its ability to hover and as a pollinator, and since the disclosure was an unexpected by-product of a reduced enthusiasm for digging, I had better tell the story from the beginning.

Separating my garden from a tarmac playground is a tall chain-link fence. I have, over the last 12 years, embedded about half of this, some 30 yards, in a hawthorn hedge, merely by transplanting the bird-sown seedlings which regularly appear in the garden. The unhedged remainder is useful as a support for climbing-plants; and runner beans, nasturtiums, morning glory, sweet peas and ornamental gourds all take their turn in relieving the blankness of the open fence.

An unwanted competitor, the great white bindweed, each year attempts to stake a claim on the same desirable site. By dint of annual trenching and some undercutting beneath the boundary, I have more or less kept the intruder at bay but total eradication is not attainable for the enemy has an unassailable stronghold for its reserve forces far beneath the tarmac.

I have often thought, particularly when seeing the large white trumpets and handsome dark foliage adorning some normally bare support such as the wire stay of a telegraph-post, that if only this weed were a trouble-free annual like its cousin, the morning glory, it would be a desirable garden plant. I like to persuade myself that it was this sneaking regard for the enemy, rather than sheer indolence, that last season led to a compromise pact in the annual boundary dispute. For about six yards I did no under-cutting, but made do with a 2-ft.-deep trench on my side that served as a defensive moat; thus the bindweed was permitted to ramp upwards but not inwards.

The result was quite spectacular, for by late July the solid wall of greenery, starred with large white blooms at 6 in. intervals, not only formed a sheltering screen for my five rows of sweet corn, but also aroused puzzled comment, and even admiration, from distant passers-by.

At dawn on several mornings from August 5 onwards, a few warblers, either chiffchaffs or willow warblers were flushed from the potato-patch, but each day it was noted that the bindweed-wall became the focus of activity once the sun got higher. Normal approach up the garden path disturbed the feeders before I could discover what they were seeking, and it was not until August 11 that I found the answer. I had made a cautious and crouching stalk through the blackcurrants to within ten feet of the site, and after a brief wait was rewarded by the sight of a chiffchaff emulating a humming-bird in front of a convolvulus trumpet. Its tail was depressed, its legs dangled, and its wings were vibrating so rapidly that they appeared as blurs rather than clear-cut shapes. At this momentary stage the tip of the beak was just within the floral trumpet, but then with a sudden probe forward the head was plunged deep into the flower. Four other blooms were similarly visited before I moved forward to investigate, and at each flower more than one probing movement was made. I found that almost every bloom harboured minute black beetles, most having five, one in each nectary at the base of the funnel.

I then remembered that in an Oxfordshire garden, almost a quarter of a century before, I had observed willow warblers feeding in exactly the same manner, and seeking similar prey, at the flowers of an evening primrose. I also recalled that on that occasion I had trapped and ringed two of the visi-tors by luring them into a cage-trap baited with a heavily infested bloom. I therefore hastily set up a trap baited with a convolvulus into which I had shaken the beetles from several others, and in less than ten minutes I had caught and ringed a chiffchaff. Just as I released it I realised the pollinating significance of this occurrence; would I have to wait yet another 25 years for another opportunity? The answer came soon after lunch, for the same bird came back for more and was retrapped.

This time I made a close examination to see if any pollen-dusting was visible, but, finding none I decided on a microscopic search. A glass slide was breathed upon and then stroked gently three times from the base of the bill to the crown. A microscopic examination revealed three spherical pollen-cells and a subsequent comparison with pollen straight from a bindweed flower showed that both samples were identical. It is probable that my specimen was more heavily dusted than this cursory inspection suggested, for from the observed mode of feeding the chin and sides of the face would be just as likely to come into contact with the anthers.

Hovering is by no means an unusual feeding-technique for warblers – it is frequently resorted to when food is inaccessible from a normal perching stance. Terminal buds on drooping twigs are often visited in this manner, but perhaps the most likely site for this energetic activity is a leafy sycamore with its usual infestation of greenfly; here the rich food supply on the undersides of the outermost leaves, and on the bottom layer of the canopy, can be reached only by hovering from below.

I am told by J. Balfour-Browne, of the British Museum (Natural History) that the beetle in the convolvulus was a *Meligithes aeneus*, a species that is both a pollen-eater and a nectar-drinker.

It was not only the national press which benefited from Bill's skill with the written word. He was a regular nature correspondent for the *Oxford Mail*, and this article, written in November 1989, was one of many he contributed:

Feathered friends get flummoxed by fog

A noticeable feature during some of the recent days of dense fog has been the almost complete cessation of bird activity.

This was first noticed at feeding sites in my garden, when, so long as the fog persisted, the usual regular customers failed to put in an appearance. Then a day or two later, when I hoped to do some birdwatching on a visit to Norfolk, even worse conditions prevailed. In the nature reserve which normally abounded with bird life in the reeds of the fen and the trees and scrub of the carr, the only birds seen – the odd blackbird, robin, wren and bluetit – were not actively feeding, but flushed from perches as we passed.

There are probably two different reasons for this immobility; firstly it is the increasing intensity of light which arouses birds from their sleep, and presumably the static birds simply are unaware that (by the clock) it is time to awake and get moving, when they cannot see the sky for fog.

The other important factor is that, in dense fog, birds are unable to navigate in their usual manner – either by noting the position of the sun or by sighting familiar landmarks.

A good illustration of this happened some years ago when on a foggy winter night the cawing of rooks from a hedge near my house attracted my attention and I found a flock roosting there. The hedge, only some ten feet high, was about a couple of miles from their traditional roost in some tall elms (which no longer exist). The obvious inference was that, unable to navigate normally, they had settled on the first site available. I recall also, another dramatic result of a sudden dense fog, this time during the autumn migration of summer visitors.

I was staying at a bird observatory off the Pembroke coast, where a daily census of the birds present was taken. On this particular day in August, after a few days of clear weather, only the usual resident species were recorded, with not a single warbler. That night the fog-horn blared and boomed continuously, and when I went out at dawn the island was enveloped in dense fog.

A warbler on my shoulder

As I walked through the bracken, birds were flushed at almost every step, and they were obviously still tired, for I had the pleasant experience of having a whitethroat settle on my head and a willow warbler perching on my shoulder.

Within the next few hours we had caught (for ringing) several hundred each of willow warbler and white-throat.

These are both nocturnal travellers when on migration, navigating by taking their bearings on stars and constellations. Of course in the prevailing conditions this was impossible, and these birds were lucky in having stumbled across solid land by chance – at such times it is known that failure to find a solid landing may result in exhausted birds dropping into the sea.

Local conservation and wildlife projects always could count on Bill's support. Here's an account he wrote for a nature reserve which was set up very close to his Charlbury home:

Blenheim Farm Nature Reserve

Thanks to the faithful gang of helpers on week-end working parties, the reserve is gradually taking shape – coarse vegetation, particularly nettles encroaching from the marginal trees and bushes, is being eliminated from the main central grassy area, and the purchase of a strimmer and other tools (thanks to donations from the Friends of the Reserve and a grant from CPRE and Shell 'Better Britain' campaign) has been welcomed by the former wielders of scythes and grass-hooks. Despite the drought, the fenced-in nursery, where seeds of local wild flowers were scattered, now provides a reservoir of a wide variety of species, such as teasel, knapweed, sorrel, moon-daisy, marjoram, St. John's wort, toadflax, cranesbills, wild basil, and, best of all, our local speciality, meadow clary. Eventually some of these will be distributed around the reserve, and, one hopes, become established despite the visitors from the adjacent rabbit-warren.

The saplings of trees and shrubs, all strictly of local native species, have also survived the dry spell with few casualties, but, amongst the established trees, almost certainly 'self-setters' and not the result of deliberate planting, I find the apples of particular interest. For the fact is, that although any wild apples are loosely classed as crab-apples, the genuine article, with its distinctive acerbic flavour, seems to be outnumbered by specimens which have some cultivated apple genes in their make-up. Thus of the four in our reserve only one, with small, yellow long-stemmed fruits, and the mouth-drying taste, is a true crab. Of the others, one, against the playing-field fence, is larger than the average crab, and a splendid cooker – it froths up like a bramley. The one near the top stile is also sweeter than a crab, whilst the fourth has large yellow, conical fruits of the codlin type – but it is pretty tasteless.

Since cultivated forms of apples far outnumber the genuine crab, it is obvious that cross-pollination from this source frequently occurs. As to the vector of these self-setters, thrown-away apple cores are one possibility, and birds seem unlikely, since even small crabs are unlikely to be swallowed whole. But once, whilst sheltering beneath an old hawthorn during a snow-storm, a marsh-tit with a tiny crab held by the stem in its beak, flew between my legs into a hollow between the buttress roots, and there in the cavity, I found a small pyramid of what presumably was to be its winter-store. But even foxes may be the unwitting sowers of crab-seed, for as David Macdonald discovered during his classic piece of research (*Running with the Fox*), apple cores are amongst the items which these carnivores with a sweet tooth are known to 'cache' by burying, for future use.

At present the ground beneath these apples is strewn with the fallen fruits, but once the bumper crop of berries – mainly hips and haws – has been stripped by hungry members of the thrush family – blackbirds, song-thrushes, mistle-thrushes, redwings and fieldfares – this reserve source of food will be eagerly exploited. Here it is interesting to note that, although blackbirds may be seen in the reserve all the year round, there may be winter-visitors, indistinguishable from our native resident population, feeding on the fallen crabs. From my immediate locality I have ringed individuals in winter which have subsequently been recovered on their home ground in Holland, Denmark, Norway, Sweden, North Germany, and Finland.

But it was his thirty years of writing Wednesday's *Guardian* Country Diary for which his work is best known and which have to feature extensively in this book. Bill kept most of his entries, and this reproduction of his first-ever entry was among them: it's reproduced here with the permission of Guardian Newspapers:

A COUNTRY DIARY
Berkshire. January 6. Last autumn I saved about a pint of pea seed and left it, spread out in a shallow bowl, to dry off in my garden shed before storage in a mouse-proof jar. Three days later I found the bowl empty. If only I had the time to undertake a complete turn-out of the shed I think I should find the peas neatly stored together, for the culprit is undoubtedly a wood mouse. There is even a faint hope that this thrifty but unintelligent rodent has stored them in a place where they will be safe from the fate for which they were intended, judging from the behaviour of one of the same species last year. Then I had left an empty flower pot inverted on a pane of glass in an open frame; during the winter I lifted the pot and found that it had been completely filled with lime seeds. They must have been dropped, one by one, through the half-inch drainage hole, and of course would have been quite inaccessible when needed.

But even if the wood mouse lacks reasoning powers, it shows a nice sense of discrimination in taste; my lodger has for some weeks now been on an apple diet, and though it has the choice of many varieties of excellent cookers it has so far touched nothing but the only eater stored in the shed. This is the dull-looking but well-flavoured Sturmer Pippin. Since it returns to the same apple night after night until only the stalk remains, it is not a wasteful pest.

Bill never failed to deliver his diary even when in very poor health following a car accident. He died at his home on 23rd November 1994 just as his countless followers were reading what was to be his last Country Diary, about one of his favourite haunts, the ancient Forest of Wychwood. Although Bill was too ill to write his last diaries, they were still his words, either dictated or, at the end, taken from one of his numerous recordings and radio programmes.

The last entry is obviously not in his personal collection – although that does include cuttings up to the beginning of November 1994 – but The Guardian did supply us with a copy, which we can reproduce here. The words were taken from one of his recordings and, appropriately enough, they are on the theme of his beloved 'Forest':

A COUNTRY DIARY

Oxfordshire: 23 Nov 1994. In 1988 Wychwood became accessible to the public. The forest goes back to pre-Norman times and was used for royal hunting of wild boars and deer, both red and fallow. Before the forest was privatised it was a royal forest and somewhere in the early 1850s there was an act of Parliament making it private and it was purchased by Lord Churchill. Prior to its privatisation, lots of people had rights of various sorts. Some had the right to gather timber, some to lop trees, but not to cut complete trees down. One of the most interesting was the right of pannage which this time of the year meant bringing livestock into the forest to feed on the fallen acorns and beechnuts. If they came to the forest today they wouldn't find any acorns, but that is another story. The livestock was chiefly pigs, and the old swine-herds used to build a hut of branches and live with their pigs. There was an interesting story that they used to have a horn which they blew at night to call their pigs into an enclosure for safety. Years ago the forest was only accessible to the public with permission of the owner. Quite a lot of local people had permission and the park which adjoins the forest and surrounds the big house was open to the public every Thursday afternoon and nearly all the local tradespeople walked through the park on their half day off; it was a long circular walk but that isn't permitted now. There was only one day in the year when the public were allowed in. Originally it was an ancient right for just one parish, Fieldtown. They had the right on Palm Sunday to go down to a certain spring to make a concoction called Spanish Liquor. It was made with medicinal liquorice, peppermint and water from the spring. When the forest was sold it became known that it was possible to gain entry on Palm Sunday and hundreds and hundreds of people came from all over England. I remember meeting people from Lancashire and Kent. There were over 1,000 on some Sundays, taking advantage of the one chance a year to look at the forest.

Like the rest of us, Bill was human and in November 1992 had decided that life was no longer worth living. As he wrote in that week's *Guardian* piece…

particularly in view of the neglected state of my garden, which was once voted equal first as the best kept in our little town, and the fact that I could no longer visit the usual sites, either by foot or by car, for inspiration for my Diaries. The most appropriate remedy (in the absence of sleeping pills, which I do not possess) seemed to be the berries of a plant which was the subject of my introduction to the Linnean system of plant nomenclature; for over eighty years ago, at the still-extant colony, Dad had very firmly pointed it out to me, deadly nightshade. Having decided that, by some means or other, I would get a botanical friend to take me to the site (provided that the apparently immune pheasants and blackbirds had not scoffed the berries first) I was suddenly pulled up by a thought – but what about your *Guardian* piece which you have to write tomorrow? And so the final solution came to nought. Many letters from readers supplied flattering encouragement to carry on and, above all, [so did] the arrival next day of two of my converts to an interest in natural history in their teenages about forty years ago, to spend several hours digging and cleaning a weedy plot. Since I write this on my eighty-seventh birthday, having received many letters and cards, phone calls and visitors, I have to realise that LIFE is still worth living.

In the next four chapters you have a chance to read a selection of WD's Country Diaries. Out of the 1500 or so of his weekly contributions, we've selected one out of each of the seasons from each of the 30 years he was writing, starting in January 1964 and finishing in November 1994, when he died.

Before you start to explore them, here's an appropriate tribute from Mrs Susan Strachan, who lives in Charlbury just opposite where Bill's house and garden used to be:

For me, reading *The Guardian* Country Diary, whilst living for years in London, was a way of keeping in touch with the changing seasons and the natural rhythms of nature. I was always drawn particularly to the

Oxfordshire pieces by W.D. Campbell. He could evoke the experiences of the countryside around him and bring them to life on the page.

I remember an article describing a winter walk by the Evenlode – probably in late December – in which he described passing a flooded field which had frozen over. A flock of lapwing were resting on the ice and the low setting sun cast a crimson glow across the ice and to the valley beyond. I have since observed this scene – possibly the field described is by the bridge on the way to Chadlington – when the trees were covered in hoar frost.

I little thought that my husband and I would come to live opposite Bill Campbell's old home. Sadly, I never met him, but I am grateful to him for the pleasure he gave me in his writings. Also, I feel it is a legacy from him that we have such an amazing variety of birds in our garden.

10

COUNTRY DIARIES – SPRING

A COUNTRY DIARY 1964

Berkshire, March 22: Although the stone-curlew failed to turn up for last week's notes, I believe that it did come in with that flash-in-the pan touch of spring. It is unlikely that it could have battled through the easterly gale and blizzard which so soon followed, yet on the morning of March 15 it was calling on the snowy downs. The information was telephoned by a farmer near whose house this fascinating bird breeds, and to such fortunate countrymen the first weird but musical calls of the stone-curlew are as welcome and significant as the sound of the first cuckoo is to others.

I missed this first of our local spring migrants since I was spending that weekend on the Oxfordshire fringe of the Cotswolds. In desperation, after having been penned indoors first by rain and then by a growing blizzard, a brief expedition was planned to a favourite patch of floodwater in the Windrush valley, just over the hills. A few wintering duck, with perhaps the chance of a Bewick's swan or newly arrived redshank, was as much as we hoped for. The site at first looked blank but sounds of at least two species of duck encouraged us to go closer – and we flushed a spoonbill. Presumably it was a weather vagrant pushed far to the west of its course by the easterly gales while en route from its tropical winter quarters to Holland. I should really have headed this article 'Oxon/Glos.,' for this rare visitor was seen over both counties.

A COUNTRY DIARY 1965

Berkshire: On the evidence gathered during over thirty years of investigation, yesterday I would have stated confidently that, given a choice between redcurrants and aphids, the lesser whitethroat would choose the dessert course every time. Today I have had it made clear to me that, while such a dogmatic assertion might be correct for thirty-three years running, it does not follow that it will be true during the thirty-fourth. Today, almost from dawn till dusk, the monotonous 'chack-chack' contact call of this warbler has come from a family party of six dispersed about my garden. They have confined their foraging almost entirely to a large (and bullfinch-barren) greengage and four rows of peas. Some thirty cage traps, baited with redcurrants and mealy aphis alternately were placed at strategic points, and the whole family has been caught (and several individuals recaught) during the course of the day. But in every case the tempting chains of currants were bypassed – I even observed one bird perched on an erect trapdoor, with what I used to think its favourite food only a few inches beneath its feet, busily engaged in taking insects from the pea-haulms.

Until a few years ago my results with chiffchaffs had been exactly in accordance with the highest authorities – ' No evidence of fruit': but since then I have repeatedly caught this warbler with berries. Sticklers for fact pointed out that this was mere circumstantial evidence, since I had not seen a chiffchaff in the act of eating berries. Today one caught in a currant-baited trap provided me with sufficient proof that fruit had passed through its digestive system – it left a huge blob of purple (blackcurrant, I suspect) on the back of my hand.

A COUNTRY DIARY 1966

Berkshire: 'All nature is so full, that that district produces the greatest variety which is most examined.' Gilbert White's famous dictum may not now be so true as it was in his day, but it is a comforting decisive factor on occasions such as early this morning, when I had risen with the intention of looking for stone curlew and wheatear on the Downs some five miles away. But a gale was blowing from the west, and my distant goal was hardly discernible against an inky sky framed in a perfect early morning rainbow. After the storm had passed I decided to be content with a stroll round the sewage-disposal works, which, since it is only two fields away, is one of my districts which is 'most examined.' Fortunately the great congregation of meadow pipits on spring passage, noted a fortnight ago, had passed on, and only a few of this species, feeding on the lawn-like grass or engaging in precocious amorous chases, were present. Thus it was easy to pick out one bird, which although obviously a pipit, was contrastingly different from the four meadow pipits within view on the same plot of grass. From its larger size, dark legs, and pale plumage with well-marked white wing-bars and pure white outer tail~feathers, I am satisfied that I have seen my first water-pipit, and the pinkish-buff flush on its breast completes the picture of this species in almost full breeding-plumage. 'Species' is hardly the correct word, since this bird is considered to be an Alpine European race of the darker rock-pipit of our own shores.

A COUNTRY DIARY 1967

Berkshire: A year ago, on the final monthly census of wintering duck, counters here and elsewhere in the Thames Valley were greeted by the song of the chiffchaff. There was no such appropriate accompaniment to stress the end-of-season nature of the task this year. After the recent gales from almost every point of the compass in turn, this was hardly expected (though gales or no gales, some small long-distance migrants got through; on March 12 both chiffchaff and sand-martins were at pits in the Reading area). Nevertheless, the tally of waterfowl told its own tale of the overlap between winter and spring. The mallard, already thinned down a month ago to 75 (compared with a winter peak of almost 400), now numbered eight, and these, significantly, were in isolated pairs. A flock of coot was still present, but consisting of a mere 50 instead of over 200. Instead of the winter raft of eight dabchick, only a pair remained, while a pair of their larger and, more spectacular cousins, the great crested grebes, had taken up breeding-residence.

The great crested grebes and the redshank are absent from this area in winter, and their arrival during the past few weeks, if only from coastal wintering-sites, is as much a sign of the beginning of spring migration as is the first chiffchaff. The barren pools, faithfully visited monthly with no reward other than a 'Nil' entry on the census-form, now have their breeding occupants – pairs of mallard, great crested grebe, and coot. Birds of both the last two species were already sitting tight on early nests. Even the rubbish-dump is now quiet, for of the thousands of gulls only three full-plumaged black-heads are left.

A COUNTRY DIARY 1968

Oxfordshire: I was pleased to discover on Palm Sunday that from one Wychwood village the traditional ritual – a pilgrimage to a spring in the forest to obtain water for making 'Spanish liquor ' – is still maintained. In my schooldays in a neighbouring market town some fifty years ago, the deep brown solution, brought to school in bottles on the next day, was already being prepared from a debased formula – the water came from the tap, the 'Spanish' could only be the thin, inch-wide flexible strips of sweetened liquorice costing a farthing for about a foot-length, whilst the peppermint flavouring could also be obtained from the sweetshop in the white tablets of 'extra strong mints'. But the purists insist that the water must be from a traditional natural source, the 'Spanish' must be the unsweetened medicinal product, and the peppermint likewise must be in the form of essence of peppermint. The fact that one local source was known as 'Lady's Well' suggests a pre-reformation Christian origin, and it is conceivable that the ingredients themselves represent biblical ' bitter herbs.' But the site where I have just renewed acquaintance with 'Spanish liquor Sunday' is a spring with a name of herbal rather than religious significance, for although the vernacular pronunciation is Uzzell, the Ordnance Survey map transcribes this as Worts Well; but what special worts or plants are commemorated in this name remains an insoluble mystery. Incidentally a search on the OS map would fail to reveal the forest village from which the recent celebrants came, for after nine hundred years of occupation they have not yet accepted the Frenchified La Felde which the Normans used – they still maintain, with sturdy Anglo-Saxon independence, that they are from Field Town.

A COUNTRY DIARY 1969

Dorset: Radipole Lake, the bird sanctuary practically in the heart of Weymouth, seems to attract more than its fair share of uncommon bird visitors. This may be partly due to natural geographical causes, but I suspect that an equally important factor is the regularity with which it is watched by both local and visiting ornithologists – and amongst the latter are those who, like myself, consider this site a compulsory halt en route to or from the Portland Bill Bird Observatory. This spring's main excitement has been a transatlantic vagrant, a Laughing Gull, and very obligingly, it was within close binocular range a few days ago when I parked at the water's edge for a belated lunch. As is usually the case with such stray wanderers, the bird was an immature in dull plumage, and I must confess that, had I not already been aware that this rarity (only the third British record) had been around for several weeks, I might not have noticed it,. Another strategic point which tends to delay travellers making for The Bill is the convenient pull-in where the muddy shore of The Fleet is near the road. The current attraction here is that former British breeding wader which has now become a rare visitor – the Kentish Plover. Unlike the gull, this bird was in full breeding plumage – and unlike almost any bird, common or otherwise, which I have ever watched, this specimen was brighter in plumage than any of the many text-book illustrations with which I am familiar.

A COUNTRY DIARY 1970

Berkshire: Although I could be certain of seeing a winter congregation of possibly well over a hundred swans by travelling to a Thames-side town a few miles away, I have nevertheless spent this chilly but sunny first morning of March in search of a herd of a mere 48, reported on a Kennet valley gravel-pit a few days ago. The reason for the excitement which these caused is that they were not the pampered and semi-domesticated beauties of the Thames, but genuine wild swans – 47 Bewick's and one Whooper, winter-visitors from the far north of Europe. Bewick's are occasional visitors to this area, but the largest party which I have ever seen together has been seven – and at that figure my local record must remain, for two Mutes were the only swans to be found on many hundreds of acres of waters scanned this morning. But the excursion was well worth while for (in contrast with monthly duck-count Sundays, when visibility is usually poor) the thousands of waterfowl present were lit up by the brilliant sunshine, as were the catkin-laden branches of hazel and alder and the orange and golden bark of willows. Thus it was easy to pick out about six goldeneye among the hundreds of tufted duck and pochard, a pair of shoveler near the few mallard, and one goosander with a dozen or so great crested grebe. Some of the latter were still in drab winter plumage, but three precocious pairs, in full breeding finery, were already engaged in their striking display-rituals.

A COUNTRY DIARY 1971

Oxfordshire: Recently, in a book about rural crafts, I came across the oft-repeated statement that the typical drystone walls of the Cotswolds are a substitute for hawthorn hedges because the latter will not flourish on the thin stony soil or on exposed uplands. On the very next morning after reading this fallacious explanation, I was presented with the evidence which, with the falling into disrepair of so many of these old field-boundaries, lies hidden in many an apparently normal mixed hedge. A merlin, attracted by the flock of finches, tree sparrows and yellowhammers feeding on a weedy patch of arable, flew off the top of a ragged hedge, and settled again some way ahead. Immediately I had a vague memory of an encounter with this winter-visiting falcon at precisely the same site about 40 years ago, but felt that my bump of location must be failing, for on the previous occasion (very memorable because it was my first-ever merlin) the bird had behaved in very much the same way, but my mental picture was of a casual retreat along the top of a drystone wall. A closer examination of the hedge vindicated my memory, for at the base the collapsed slabs of limestone of the original boundary could still be seen. Perching birds had sown hawthorn, bramble, briar, elder, blackthorn and ivy, whilst the wind had drifted seeds of old man's beard, ash and sycamore to form the present natural successor to the original artifact.

A COUNTRY DIARY 1972

Oxfordshire: It would be interesting to discover through some random sampling of public opinion what scent is most commonly associated with April. It might well turn out that the majority of answers would be in the 'don't know' category, since in my experience (backed by numerous experiments with children which seemed to show that mint, thyme, sage, and marjoram all smelt of chewing gum), the modern nose is unable to differentiate between very distinctive aromas. But, for the country dweller I would imagine that, among flowers, either the primrose or the wild sweet violet would top the poll, and that hyacinths would rank high among urban gardeners or frequenters of public parks. The scent of warmed earth dampened by April showers – a paradoxical blend of freshness and mustiness – would undoubtedly be high in the scale for both town and country. But for me one insignificant little flower, the moschatel or town hall clock, epitomises April, but its peculiar seasonal affinities seem to escape general attention, simply because it is so inconspicuous. The clump on otherwise bare ground beneath some ancient beeches, although in full bloom, looks remarkably like the seedlings of some umbelliferous plant such as celery. But the paler green flower-heads above the foliage, each arranged in a cube with four petalled flowers on the vertical faces and a five-petalled bloom on the crown, have a scent (very fleeting, and dependent on atmospheric conditions) which for me is that of April; the sweetness of nectar is there, but it is intermingled with the musky, almost fungal smell of earth after an April shower.

A COUNTRY DIARY 1973

Oxfordshire: A few miles from here, on the outskirts of a charming Cotswold village, snowdrops are at present adorning the roadside verges; investigation suggests that they have gradually spread from woodland through which the road cuts, and doubtless, as with many drifts of apparently wild daffodils and winter aconites in similar situations, the plants are not wholly wild, but the result of deliberate naturalisation. Modern botanists seem less certain than their Victorian forerunners as to the status of the snowdrop, for, as far as I can discover, most of the latter seem to accept that the plant was a long established alien, but the most authoritative British flora of today admits the possibility that the snowdrop, although most frequently occurring as an introduced species, may be truly indigenous in the extreme South-west and West of Britain. To me the most significant factor in support of the theory that it is a comparatively recent introduction to Southern and Midland England is that Shakespeare, who mentions the introduced crocus in his long catalogue of wild and garden plants, makes no mention of the snowdrop; and it is inconceivable that such a strikingly conspicuous and precocious flower would have escaped his attention. According to the *OED*, the first known written allusion to the snowdrop does not occur until 1664 – some half a century too late for Shakespeare.

A COUNTRY DIARY 1974

Oxfordshire: Many pounds of peanuts have passed through the bags of red plastic netting since they were suspended from my Scots pine at the beginning of last October, and I ought to feel disappointed at their failure to attract the siskins for which they were intended. But, as I reported early last December, the feeding site has proved of great interest in enabling me to form some idea of the numbers of other birds which were immediately attracted to them. At that time I mentioned that one fact which had emerged was that almost daily different birds, or parties of birds, were involved, and that the apparently regular visitors were in fact mainly random wanderers. This pattern of visitation still continues, and the score of individuals marked and thus identified now stands at exactly 600 blue tits, 300 greenfinches, 120 great tits, 10 coal tits, and one solitary willow tit. A very tentative estimate (based on the proportion of ringed birds which have been recaught during the same period) suggests that the blue tit population within feeding range of my garden is around 2,500 during the winter months, and one wonders whether this sample is representative of its general numerical status. Since a very high proportion of small birds succumb during their first winter, the annually growing amount of nourishment obtained from bird tables during this critical period must surely have reduced the risk in the case of the fearless and adaptable blue tit. The chances of reaching the ripe old age of 11, as my record-holding individual did, should now be much greater.

A COUNTRY DIARY 1975

Oxfordshire: In a normal season (if such a thing exists in our variable climate) summer migrants appear in a fairly predictable pattern – chiffchaffs, wheatears and sand martins in the first half of March, with a gap of several weeks before the arrival of willow warblers, swallows, yellow wagtails and cuckoos. This spring's pattern of arrival seems to suggest that the overdue species have dallied somewhere on the way – presumably awaiting an improvement in both wind direction and temperature – for within the past ten days, coinciding with the milder westerly weather, there has been an influx of all the species listed above. Thus my first chiffchaff's song was not heard until April 15, almost a month later than average, whereas that of the willow warbler followed within twelve hours. Although swallows were plentiful over some gravel pit pools a few miles away on April 13, my regular residents did not appear until April 19. I was pretty sure as to the identity of the cock, for he settled and sang on his favourite perch. I then realised that the window of the garden shed needed opening another notch to make access to the nesting site easier, and then the identity of the bird was made even more certain, for he zipped past my ear into the shed whilst I still stood on the ladder. Arrival dates for this particular bird (taking the first visit to the old nest as the criterion) have in the past four years varied from April 10 last year to as late as May 1 in 1971.

A COUNTRY DIARY 1976

Oxfordshire: One of the few constant factors in our otherwise unpredictable climate is the lengthening of the days from the third week in March onward, and it is generally accepted that this is the main external stimulus which brings birds into breeding condition. As usual a few attempted to 'jump the gun' this season, notably a dunnock which had finished its nest and lined it with cowhair by March 7, and two blackbirds which had completed nests by March 18. On the latter date a blackbird was already incubating her clutch high in the rafters of my neighbour's barn. Normally, once a nest is completed and lined, one expects the bird to start laying almost immediately, but, apart from the sheltered exception, each of my early birds seemed to lose interest in thc nests which had been so hurriedly constructed, and although I continued to glance at their empty state daily as I passed, I finally came to the conclusion that they had been deserted But, just 24 days after the nest had been completed, the dunnock began to lay, and both blackbirds did the same after a delay of 22 days. I can only conclude that a continuous series of very frosty nights in some way inhibited the breeding urge of the birds in the open hedges, whilst the bird in the cosy shed experienced no such setback; its fully fledged young were exploring my garden several days ago.

A COUNTRY DIARY 1977

Oxfordshire: During a brief spell of sunshine on March 21 in spite of a wind approaching gale force and little above freezing point, two sand martins suddenly appeared over the water at Blenheim and, after about 10 minutes of hawking over the waves, apparently moved on, or sought shelter, for I failed to find them again during a circuit of the lake. It seems odd that this bird, the smallest of our three native swallows, should invariably arrive so much earlier than the swallow and house martin. Although widely reported since the middle of the month, the chiffchaff has so far eluded me, and an expedition to some gravel-pits, where I usually hear and see my first among the flowering twigs of the sallows, has today (March 22) proved fruitless in this respect, but rewarding nevertheless. During a wet and very windy walk little of interest could be found on the water, except for the last of the winter-visiting wildfowl – about 10 wigeon and a pair of goosander – and then, just as I was about to leave, a merlin crossed my path and hovered momentarily over a bare expanse of unfilled ground before disappearing round a headland. But, as I scanned the area with my glasses, I discovered that beneath the hovering-point the ground was alive with small birds. As expected they turned out to be mainly pied wagtails, well over 100, with a good sprinkling of reed buntings, almost entirely cocks, and meadow pipits. But among them, while searching for a possible white wagtail among the pied, I was delighted to find my second punctual summer migrant – a cock wheatear in splendid peach-breasted breeding-plumage.

A COUNTRY DIARY 1978

Oxfordshire: Recently, on an early morning trip into The Forest (as Wychwood is always known locally) the just-perceptible needle-point trills of goldcrests could be heard from a coniferous plantation, and since an unusually large gathering seemed to be indicated, I walked slowly down the ride which seemed to lead to the focus of the high-frequency chorus. But a careful search of the likeliest site – the tops of larches, spruce and pines – only revealed the presence of two birds. These diverted my attention from my first intention, for it suddenly struck me that, although I must have watched goldcrests feeding in conifers hundreds of times before, a characteristic feature of foraging behaviour among branches, although now recalled, had not previously impressed me. This was the ability, demonstrated repeatedly as I watched, for a goldcrest to reach a much lower level not by normal flight, but by a miniature parachute-drop – an ability which is shared by the wood-warbler. But this side-tracking of my interest was soon corrected by the realisation that the goldcrest calls were coming, not from the tree-tops, but from a nearby clearing strewn with clumps of 'browse' – the trimmings of tops and side-branches from recent felling operations. Here I counted nine, some hovering above the heaps, and some actually disappearing into them in wren-fashion. I was racking my brains as to what could be the attraction in such a seemingly sterile habitat when the sun came out, and, literally in a flash, the problem was resolved: spiders, for the whole area was criss-crossed with scintillating single strands of silk.

A COUNTRY DIARY 1979

Oxfordshire: Regardless of the unseasonable weather, woodcock began their spectacular evening patrols up and down our local woodland rides in the first week in March – an obvious indication that lengthening daylight, even in the absence of increasing temperature, is all that is needed to trigger off this activity. It was almost a fortnight after receiving this information from the head-keeper that I was able to witness this performance myself, and then, on the first occurrence of suitable weather, I took up my position at the junction of several rides just before sunset. For the first ten minutes or so nothing was to he heard but the clamour of what must have been hundreds of pheasants crowing and fluttering as they went to roost, and the crash-landings of wood-pigeons as they did likewise in the pines in whose lee I was sheltering. Then, just as a tawny owl added its more soothing voice to the cacophony of the cock-pheasants rashly advertising their individual lodgings for the night, and as the last glow of pink lit up the horizon, from somewhere over the pines behind me came the call of a woodcock – a peculiar mixture of sounds suggestive of both squeaking and twittering clicks. Then the caller passed right overhead, close enough for me to hear its other totally different call – a hoarse, croaking grunt, invariably accompanied by a slowing down in flight approaching a hover or stall. This ritual demarcation of the breeding-territory by the cock is known as 'roding,' and I am surprised to learn, on consulting my *OED*, that the term is 'of obscure origin.' Since the same term is (or was) used for the regular evening flight-paths of wildfowl from sea to landward, I had always assumed that 'rode' was merely a variant spelling of 'road,' indicating the following of a regular track. On my way home, at a point where the narrow road transects woodland, having had the satisfaction of witnessing roding over the rides, I had the added pleasure of meeting another bird actually roding up and down the road, or, as Shakespeare spelt it, the rode.

A COUNTRY DIARY 1980

Oxfordshire: On a recent sunny morning, in well-treed open parkland, I became aware of a persistent chorus of birdsong from a clump of ancient trees about a quarter of a mile away. Although the general effect of confused twittering, with occasional more musical warblings and whistlings, seemed vaguely familiar, I was at first at a loss to put a name to the species responsible. Then, as I drew near enough to spot scores of thrush-sized birds in the crown of the nearest lime, and similar parties excitedly flitting from crown to crown of the old beeches, oaks and sycamores further ahead, I recalled the first occasion on which I had become familiar with this sound – over 30 years ago, when a redwing roost was in a copse near my house in Berkshire. Night after night, at this time of the year, they sang their vespers before darkness set in.

I came across a similar and even more widespread gathering of these birds in tree-tops of the forest bordering the park, but then they were silent, apart from the occasional squeak or squawk.

It seems likely that this communal outburst of subsong is preparation for the full song on their return to home ground in Scandinavia or Iceland. But not only redwings and fieldfares will be drawing to the end of their winter stay – many of our winter blackbirds are also visitors. One such, a female which I ringed in my garden in the winter of 1975, was found dead, entangled in fruit-netting, 1350 miles away to the north-east near Kuopi, Finland, early last October.

A COUNTRY DIARY 1981

Oxfordshire: On one of the glorious sunny days in the middle of this month I witnessed two items of behaviour which, in human terms, seemed to suggest that they were due to mistaken identity, although in each case the creatures involved were quite distinctly different. I was surveying the garden for butterflies when I spotted my first small white of the year busily chasing a female brimstone. At first I thought this was just a momentary affair, but for several minutes the smaller white butterfly persistently kept in close contact with – sometimes actually touching – the larger and brighter brimstone. Since the white was a male, and the female brimstone is of a very pale yellow, I can think of no other explanation than that the former, newly emerged and unfamiliar with females of the correct species, was 'having a go' at the first pale female which he encountered. As I watched the pair zig-zagging around, my attention was diverted by the chuckling call of a cock black-bird on the roof, and found that the bird, its beak stuffed with what I believe were leather-jackets (cranefly larvae), seemed to be intent on disposing of its load to a bird hopping on the roof a few feet in front of it. I assumed the latter was one of the youngsters which had left the nest in my neighbour's garden a few days previously – but the object of its solicitude turned out to be an adult starling. The latter seemed embarrassed rather than alarmed, and retreated up the slope a few feet at a time, as the blackbird advanced. Then the performance continued along the roof-ridge, and at the eaves the starling flew, still pursued by its would-be benefactor. In this case a plausible explanation is that the blackbird's brood (which left the nest prematurely) had come to grief – I found the remains of one of them – and that the cock bird was still driven by the instinctive urge to feed birds of roughly the same size and colour in its territory.

A COUNTRY DIARY 1982

Oxfordshire: Somewhat belatedly – precisely three months after the event – a reader has written taking me to task for admitting, in my Diary (December 23), that I had cut sprigs of berried holly for indoor decoration. He found it 'discomforting that an avowed country lover should put domestic Christmas decorations before the needs of wildlife,' and makes a plea that we should 'leave the natural holly for the benefit of wildlife, and make do with plastic holly for the hedonistic British Christmas.' It is also alleged in this criticism that I had praised my own 'foresight in gathering in my Christmas holly before the fieldfares could appease their hunger.'

I disclaim any such prophetic foreknowledge of what was to follow, for when I gathered my dozen or so sprigs, bearing perhaps a total of less than 100 berries, the weather was still mild. In a normal winter, these berries are an unimportant item of bird diet, and indeed, more often than not, some or all of the crop may remain uneaten and withering even when the bloom for next year's berries is appearing. Now, whilst the ounce or so of possible fieldfare food was out of circulation in my house, I trudged several times a day through knee-deep snow to a corner of a field about 200 yards away where I was keeping a patch cleared specifically for feeding fieldfares and other thrushes; and here, with many pounds of spare apples (always stored for just such a contingency) I estimate that I repaid them at least a thousandfold for what amounted to a brief borrowing of a tiny amount of their natural food. As to the offending holly behind the pictures, it came down and was burnt on Twelfth Night but the berries had been stripped off first, and duly reached their rightful consumers alongside the apples. And what did I get as my reward? – only uncomfortably strapped-up ribs, after slipping whilst hoisting a can of warm water over the gate en route to thaw my feeding-patch.

A COUNTRY DIARY 1983

Oxfordshire: In most cases dormancy in the comparatively few members of our native fauna which hibernate is not as profound as that of creatures in colder climes, for even extreme examples such as dormice and bats may re-awaken, if only temporarily, when spring-like temperatures occur in our unpredictable winters. This year my first example of this response was provided by a peacock butterfly on the wing on January 19, followed by another on an even sunnier day just a week later. During this period also I heard of a hedgehog wide-awake and actively foraging in a local garden, and I saw my first squashed road casualty of this species during the same fine spell. Ladybirds also emerged during that brief touch of spring, as did a few hive-bees. But on the glorious first of March a more general awakening of these two insects was noticeable, the ladybirds coming to the surface from the clumps of aubrieta beneath which they had been sheltering and the bees busy amongst the crocuses. But it is noticeable that the bumble-bee is not amongst these early awakeners. Only the queens of these survive the winter by hibernation, and presumably their solitary existence then in some mouse hole, old bird's nest or nest box, as opposed to the communal warmth of colonial bees, induces a more complete state of dormancy. In my experience the queen bumbles seem to synchronise their first appearance with that of the first abundant supply of pollen and nectar provided by the blossoming of the sallow-catkins, which locally should be at its height by the appropriate date of Palm Sunday.

A COUNTRY DIARY 1984

Oxfordshire: Hazel catkins are now turning brown and dropping, while those of the alder are just beginning to open, flecking the former dull purple hue with yellow. This early flowering, long before the leaves appear, makes sense in the case of such subjects, since their pollen is wind-borne and more likely to reach female flowers before leaves get in the way. But there seems to be no such obvious explanation for the winter blooming of more highly developed plants with flowers which produce nectar. In this category we have few native species, but two of them – the stinking hellebore and the spurge laurel (*Daphne laureola*) – are at present in bloom locally. Since both have green flowers and those of the latter are hidden beneath the canopy of dark leathery leaves, they rely on scent to attract pollinating insects. The daphne flowers often seem odourless by day, but in suitable atmospheric conditions emit a sweet, musky scent towards dusk, and one assumes that winter moths are the expected visitors. In the case of the hellebore the bitter scent – not so objectionable as the epithet stinking suggests – has been found to be highly attractive to bees, and the chemical involved is also present in the flowers of some crocus and broom species. In my garden the pink, sweetly scented blossoms of *Viburnum x bodnantense* have adorned a large bush since late October; a clump of a deep purple form of *Helleborus orientale* has been in full bloom since Christmas Day; and a small patch of that lovely little iris which gardeners stubbornly refuse to call by its ugly new specific name – *Iris unguicularis* instead of the old *I. stylosa* – produced its first blooms on November 28 and yielded what may be its last, the 102nd, on February 9. All these winter-bloomers have a very protracted season of flowering, thus spreading the chances from visiting bees and moths in occasional milder spells.

A COUNTRY DIARY 1985

Oxfordshire: One of the least noticed phenomena of spring re-awakening is the appearance of the Roman snail out and about after its long period of hibernation. During the latter state this snail, as is the case with its commoner garden relative, hides away in some cranny and then seals its entrance against predatory intruders during its dormancy. But whereas the garden pest merely forms a thin parchmenty seal across the opening, the Roman snail uses the lime of its environment to form a hard stony layer as its operculum. On a recent visit to see if my favourite colony of sweet violets was in bloom (and it was, in great variety of shades of blue and mauve, but with white predominating) I noticed what I took to he an empty shell of this local speciality protruding from the leaf-litter amongst the violets, but on picking it up discovered that it was occupied by an active specimen. This was a hundred yards or so away from the stony embankment which is the nearest habitat, and therefore I took a walk to count how many I could find on the stretch where I found over fifty last spring. I had walked about a quarter of a mile without success, and then found my first specimen. But it was still in the solidly sealed state, and apparently had been dislodged by a minor landslip during the thaw. It would seem therefore, that the re-awakening of this species is random rather than synchronised, and since the main colony is on a north-west facing bank, whereas the one active specimen was open to the sun, it is probably the ambient temperature which decides when the limy door becomes detached to free the occupant.

A COUNTRY DIARY 1986

Oxfordshire: For many years I had sought in vain for a well-known (or at least much-quoted) example of insect protective mimicry – the pupa of a beetle which closely resembles the seed-pods of the figwort among which it rests. Then, quite by chance, I found it abounding in my garden, not on one of our native figworts, but on the naturalised alien species, the yellow figwort (*Scrophularia vernalis*).

I have just been reminded of this incident, with a similar deflation of my self-esteem, while engaged in cutting out dead wood from the numerous victims of the winter. Some years ago I was surprised to find that the suckers arising from that lovely shrub-rose, Roseraie de l'Hay, were completely thornless, and on inquiry of the supplier learned that a thorn-less variety of the dogrose was one of the stocks in use for budding. Ever since, I have searched for a wild specimen of the same unarmed type, but considered it unlikely that such a mutation would survive the attention of grazing animals. But the propensity for such abnormal and disadvanta-geous 'sports' must exist in many prickly subjects, as is demonstrated by the numerous thornless cultivars of the bramble family now available to gardeners. Sixteen years ago, on taking over my present plot, I allowed a seedling elder to remain in an out of the way corner, and soon after a seedling dogrose appeared beneath it. Last year the rose blooms adorned the crown of the elder, now some 20 feet high. Neither had needed any attention until recently, when I found that the main stem of the rose, now a straight pole almost two inches in diameter, was dead. Arming myself with stout hedging gloves, I prepared to saw it off at the base, but as I sepa-rated the still living basal shoots, I realised that the job could be done barehanded – I had at last met with my first genuine wild thornless briar.

A COUNTRY DIARY 1987

Oxfordshire: Until about 60 years ago, red squirrels were plentiful in Wychwood; then came the invasion and population explosion of the grey aliens, and within a few years the reds – one of which used to venture into our cottage to clean up the cat's plate – had disappeared. Naturally one concluded that, either through aggression by the larger species or perhaps the transference of some disease of which the greys were immune carriers, the newcomers were directly responsible for the elimination of their more attractive cousins. But research has ruled out either of these hypotheses; it seems that the red population was declining rapidly even before the spread of the greys, and the latter, more adaptable to habitat and in feeding habits, made their all too successful takeover. Viewers of a recent BBC 'Wildlife on One' programme will have gained an insight into the current research on the red squirrel population of the Isle of Wight, a grey-free haven for our genuine Squirrel Nutkin. As a result of such studies, aided by modern techniques such as radio-tagging, but still dependent on old-fashioned all-the-year-round fieldwork, Jessica Holm has produced a comprehensive book about both species, with a preliminary section on other members of the family. (*Squirrels*, Whittet Books, 18 Anley Road, London W14 0BY, £5.95. The text has a light touch but is packed with serious information.) [Price was £7.99 in 2003 – editor.]

A COUNTRY DIARY 1988

Oxfordshire: Recently, during a discussion concerning the weather and gardening prospects, an old local acquaintance of mine expressed the opinion that there was little danger of imminent frosts, because 'The moon 'ave got too fur round for that.' This conviction that frosts were likely under a full moon in winter and spring probably contains a grain of truth, for when the moon is most obvious in its full splendour the sky is likely to be cloudless, and in such clear conditions prolonged loss of heat by radiation from the ground will lead to a frost by dawn. But this recent proof that this old piece of weather lore still persists caused me to recall my first and very memorable introduction to it. This was about some 50 odd years ago, at about this season, when, during a protracted cold spell, farmers and gardeners were longing for warmer conditions. I met Charlie, a smallholder, as I passed the village pub at turning-out time, and inevitably we discussed the weather prospects. Emphatically driving home his belief by thumping the ground with his hefty black-thorn stick, he declared this old piece of weather-lore: 'We shan't get no sort of weather as long as that bloody moon 'angs over they vicarage elms.' The elms have gone the way of their kind, but whenever I pass the site I have a confused, and of course completely false, mental picture of a bloody moon, instead of the silvery full moon shining through the twigs on that night.

A COUNTRY DIARY 1989

Oxfordshire: Hereabouts the first summer migrant to arrive is usually the chiffchaff in mid-March, closely followed by the first wheatears and sand martins. But on seeing the first of the expected pioneer species examining the precocious greenery of my Canary-bird rose just outside the window on March 3, I reluctantly decided that I could not count this as my earliest-ever record, since this winter there have been a few records of chiffchaffs over-wintering in the county. But my opinion was swayed in the other direction when I heard that, on the same date, chiffchaffs were seen, and in one case heard in song, at two sites in my neighbourhood. Confirmation that this exceptionally mild winter has brought about an abnormally early arrival of migrants has come from the Bird Observatory at Portland Bill, for a 'phone call to the warden revealed that not only chiffchaffs, but also wheatears and sand martins had begun to arrive in the first week of March and, nearer home, six sand martins were recorded at Farmoor Reservoir on March 11. As to winter visitors, the Scottish provenance of our local visitation of siskins is further confirmed by news of my second 'control' – a bird ringed at Dingwall last April. An interesting feature of the current situation is that for the past few weeks, not parties, but singletons, have come to my peanut bags, and that, of the last 13 caught, 12 have been males. It is well established that in some migratory species, such as continental chaffinches and pochard, the females travel further west or south to winter quarters, and one wonders whether, after the first influx of mixed sexes, the female siskins behave in the same way. An alternative explanation could be that the cock-birds, now passing through almost daily, have left the wintering flocks, and are on their way north to stake out claims for breeding-territories on their home-ground, for with most migratory species this is the usual procedure.

A COUNTRY DIARY 1990

Oxfordshire: On a recent sunny morning, on a sudden impulse perhaps due to the presence of three brimstones and a comma on the wing, I took an hour's break from my last belated piece of digging to visit a spinney skirting the Evenlode, with the hope of finding the local rarity, the yellow star of Bethlehem (*Gagea lutea*), in bloom. As usual, having passed patches of moschatel (the town hall clock), wood anemones, primroses and early dog violet in bloom, and fully erect flowers of the pallid parasitic toothwort springing from the roots of hazels, my eyes were glued to the ground to find the first specimen of this charming, but easily overlooked, little beauty – as with other elusive flowers, such as some of the smaller orchids, the finding of the first is crucial to 'get one's eye in,' and from then on discovery becomes easy. But on this occasion, at a point where the colony begins, my first was well above eye-level – prominent on the top of a slab of soil on the roots of a willow uprooted by the gales. Thereafter, along a walk of about a hundred yards right on the edge of the brook, I counted 56 in full bloom, some on the rich deposit of silt left by the floods, but others, hidden amongst the dog's mercury and the similarly-coloured lesser celandines, well up on the slope of the spinney. For good measure, during this annual survey, background music was provided by the continuous drumming of a great spotted woodpecker, just as it was on my last year's visit.

A COUNTRY DIARY 1991

Portland Bill, Dorset: I have been coming here, with a few exceptions, twice yearly, at spring and autumn migration times, for the last 30 years, but the earlier visit this time was not so much in expectation of greeting precocious pioneers such as chiffchaffs and wheatears, but to celebrate the thirtieth anniversary of the conversion of the old lighthouse to a bird observatory and field centre. About 50 supporters turned up, and, after a convivial evening meal, ornithological gossip continued into the small hours. A somewhat embarrassing feature of the gathering was that several of the party recognised me, but I could not recall their names – simply because faces now adorned by greying beards had, at my last encounter, been those of teenagers. Foul weather, with the fog-horn's ear-splitting blasts non-stop day and night, did not favour bird movement, but despite the conditions, one migrant, the wheatear, came up to expectation, for daily, during my four-day stay, small influxes occurred, and it was interesting to note that they seemed to be in a hurry to move on, for although a party of 11 had been seen early one morning, by late afternoon only ones or twos were noted. The only other small summer migrant which I spotted was the first sandwich tern of the season – a record supported by the appearance on the same day of one at Brownsea Island. But what impressed me more than anything else was the erosive power of the sea. I went to do a sea-watch at The Bill, and intended to stand on a platform of rock in front of the obelisk – and found that it no longer existed, and that that face of the erection was flush with the sea. Incidentally, I have frequently had to correct the notion from casual passers-by with whom I have chatted whilst doing a sea-watch at the obelisk, that the 'T. H.' on its landward face commemorates Thomas Hardy, but since it is accompanied by the date 1844, their chronology is at fault, as he was then only a four-year-old. The initials stand for Trinity House, and the obelisk was a navigational marker.

A COUNTRY DIARY 1992

Oxfordshire: Hawthorns were showing green leaves along the ring-roads around Oxford in the first week of this month, and the usual patches are in full leaf. I once toyed with the idea that the warmth generated by continuous traffic was responsible for this earliness, but since, year after year, the precocity is confined to the same plants I have come to the conclusion (backed by information from a reader) that amongst the plants imported from the continent for planting along the new roads, were specimens of an early-leafing clone. Another roadside hedge-plant which annually causes false claims for exceptional earliness is now in bloom – this is the cherry-plum, regularly, and erroneously, reported as early-flowering blackthorn. This exists locally not only as a hedge-plant, but in one site, as a clump of ancient standard specimens, and I am told that they are just as floriferous as those in the hedge. Bees and other insects have been active and a bumper crop of golden, purple or red little plums is indicated. I can still find no explanation for the use of this plum as a hedge-plant since its lack of thorniness is far inferior to our native blackthorn as impenetrable barriers to livestock, and one can only conclude that, in warmer climatic conditions, it was grown for its edible fruit. The characteristic which separates this plum from blackthorn is not only its earliness but also the fact that the leaves open with the blossoms, whereas in the blackthorn the flowers appear on the bare stems. A recent visit to Farmoor reservoirs proved almost blank as to birds present – only tens of common waterfowl such as mallard and tufted duck, and, in fact, the commonest species was the winter-visiting golden-eye, of which about 50 were present. A visit to the gravel-pit pools a few miles away revealed that mallard, tufted duck, pochard, teal and black-headed gulls were still abundant, so maybe Farmoor had been deserted on account of the exposure of its open acreage to the recent almost gale-force winds.

A COUNTRY DIARY 1993

Oxfordshire: All winter I have been longing to see the annual gathering of golden plovers in either of two adjacent fields bordering a busy road on the outskirts of Witney. My only opportunities have occurred when a friend with similar interests transports me periodically to the traditional site. Although the birds had been reported at this site, they were never there when we passed. But on a recent sunny morning, my friend rang to say that the birds were there, and that he would pick me up to see them. As we got near the site our hopes faded, for in the distance we could see, high up, a mixed flock of birds which were obviously peewits in the usual line-abreast formation, followed by a less organised mob of smaller and pointed-winged flock assumed to be the hoped-for goldies, so that it seemed that once more we had been foiled in our expectation. On arrival at the site, about 100 lapwings were already settled, accompanied by about 20 black-headed gulls and only four goldies. As we watched, both lapwings and golden plovers continued to arrive, until eventually about 300 of the former and about 200 of the latter had assembled. Although almost all of the gulls had assumed the brown-headed plumage belying their name, it was noticeable that only one of the goldies showed signs of breeding plumage – black appearing on the breast. Since my friend had recently returned from Ayrshire where he found goldies still present, we assumed that our regular local visitors are from further north; and at the end of their stay, which may be as late as the first week in April, it is noticeable that a high proportion of the birds have the more extensive black plumage of breast and neck typical of northern birds from as far afield as Iceland. I am puzzled by the presence of the gulls, for although eventually they reveal their intention by stealing food from the plovers, this seems a very chancy source of food when compared with that available to thousands of their kind scavenging at the refuse dump close by.

A COUNTRY DIARY 1994

Oxfordshire: Once again weathermen and the media have assured us that spring began on March 21; and again I assert that this is nonsense. As I have pointed out before, each season occupies three months of the year – the quarters. If March 21 is the beginning of spring, the season will end around June 21, which is midsummer which suggests that the first half of summer occurs in springtime.

A few nights ago I awoke in the early hours with a vague notion that some small creature was moving in the room. I switched on the bedside light and there was a small bird circling round just beneath the ceiling. From time to time it perched on the shade of an unlit overhead light, and occasionally disappeared through the open door into the passage leading to other rooms with open doors. But it returned again and again, but because I could only see shape and not colour, I could not identify it – from its long tail I nearly decided that it must be a pied wagtail, but then realised that it was not large enough. The only possible point of entry was an upper window in my bedroom which was only two or three inches ajar. Finally the bird disappeared and I switched off the light and went to sleep. Next morning I searched every available room for the intruder but finding no trace almost convinced myself that I had had a very realistic dream. Two days later I found the corpse of a longtailed tit beneath a cupboard in another room. The precise identification gave me a clue to the possible explanation for the fatal visit. Longtailed tits methodically examine windows to search for insects and spiders along the woodwork and metal strips holding the glass and I guess that in examining one strip which contains an open window in its centre, they willy-nilly enter the room. I came to this conclusion last summer when on three occasions tits of this species were fluttering around in my glass conservatory, and that the only possible entrance was by a window slightly ajar. These were luckier, as I caught and released them.

11

COUNTRY DIARIES – SUMMER

A COUNTRY DIARY 1964

Berkshire: 'Two hundred and fifty dollars for a beetle – as large as my fist, it is true, yet nought but a beetle after all.' This comment on the beetle-mania then current was made by Audubon about 130 years ago. Topical events, both on Merseyside and in my garden, have brought the reference to mind. Stag-beetles, huge by British standards even if not fist-sized, have been much in evidence during the last few days, and although neither hirsute nor vocal, their alarming appearance has been known to cause high-pitched screams and near-hysteria. The male, some two inches long including his antler-like mandibles, looks both grotesque and formidable, particularly when he rears up and waves his toothed pincers in a threatening manner. But in flight, as many have been lately, this creature can evoke even more alarm and consternation, for there seems to be something unnatural about the apparition of a heavy, mail-clad insect, with jaws apparently at the ready, zooming in drunken flight in broad daylight. The basal section of a fair-sized lime trunk, which I have used for some years as a chopping-block, is one of the sources from which these harmless beetles emerge each summer, and tunnelling in the rotting wood there are now the 3-year-old grubs which will produce next year's hatch. These larvae, as large as the top two joints of my index finger, must endure truly seismic shocks whenever I split logs or sharpen stakes, but the demolition work proceeds steadily, so that the block has been considerably reduced in height during the last few years, and now stands on a four-inch layer of peaty frass – all that remains of the wood once it has passed through a very specialised digestive system.

A COUNTRY DIARY 1965

Berkshire: Judging from the number of breeding pairs in my immediate neighbourhood – at least seven within 150 yards of my house – this has been an excellent season for that welcome summer visitor, the spotted flycatcher. Most of the broods have already flown, but for some weeks the speckled juveniles (the only truly 'spotted' flycatchers) will be fed, and gradually learn to live up to their name, in comparatively restricted areas around the nesting-sites. I am always amazed that this bird so often chooses human environments for nesting, for in my experience it never accepts the presence of the rightful owners of the territory (as will robin, swallow and the thrushes). Indeed, even in the open woodland which is its natural habitat, it would easily be overlooked but for its vociferous expressions of resentment at human approach. The nest under the eaves of the garden shed was overflowing with five full-grown young early this morning, but after breakfast the mixture of hissing and buzzing from a parent which flew round my ears as I walked beneath an apple tree some ten yards away, told its own story, and a glance at the nest revealed only two spotted heads projecting from the shallow box; so it seems that tomorrow I shall be able to get on with my gardening without feeling that I am an intruder.

Now that it is safe to do so without endangering nesting success, I have caught some of the adults and identified them. One of my garden pair bred near the same site in 1963, and two of the birds which nested near the brook also nested there last year.

A COUNTRY DIARY 1965

Gloucestershire: On a recent visit to Bourton-on-the-Water, I was very interested to see that magnificent bird, the quetzal, freely flying in a spacious replica of a sub-tropical habitat (in which also a pair of fruit-eating South American woodpeckers were so well established that they were busily excavating a nesting-hole). But what made the day memorable occurred before I had paid my money and passed through the turnstile to the bird-garden. In the shallow water of the Windrush, unobserved by the steady flow of visitors on the footwalk a few yards away, a bird, which at first I almost dismissed as a bathing starling, suddenly walked into deeper water, and could be plainly watched walking and pecking on the river-bed. Even if it had not emerged to perch and preen barely five yards from where I watched, thus enabling me to see its pure white breast and chestnut belly, its behaviour alone would have been sufficient to establish its identity as a dipper, for no other British perching-bird has developed this ability to exploit a most unlikely feeding-niche.

In the clear water it was possible to note that the bird was actually walking or running, and not swimming; the underwater action, consisting of erratic darting hither and thither, with occasional slight wing-flicks, was very reminiscent of the terrestial activities of a pied wagtail on a lawn. Although the dipper is usually regarded as a bird of Highland streams, odd pairs do occasionally breed in lowland areas – provided that swift-running water is available. I knew two breeding-sites in this same area many years ago, and since then breeding has occurred occasionally in West Oxfordshire.

A COUNTRY DIARY 1967

Berkshire: The dry turf on the bank at the entrance to one of our most popular local trackways on the Downs is now studded with colour. The individual flowers responsible for this show are miniature, and only the massing of the shoots into mats or cushions up to a foot in diameter draws attention to their presence. But although the general impression, at first sight, is that about half a dozen different species are in bloom, a closer look reveals that the colourful patchwork is due to the blossoming of only two plants – milkwort and horseshoe vetch. The latter is of an invariable deep gorse-yellow, but the milkworts range from pure white, through mauves and a milky off-white, to blues of varying intensity.

In his *Herball* of 1597 John Gerard listed six of these colour varieties as distinct species – including one of 'an overworn ill-favoured colour' which I think must have been the rather dingy mauve variety. But although Gerard was undoubtedly a plagiarist and not too scrupulous about recording ancient botanical mumbo-jumbo as personally observed facts, his description of the milkwort leads me to picture him, on his hands and knees, examining his native subjects at close quarters. – 'The flower grows at the top of a blewe colour, fashioned like a little bird, with wings, tail and body, only to be discovered by those who do observe the same.' An even more striking variability, since the changes are rung on form as well as colour, is currently demonstrated in a meadow where the green-winged orchid abounds; I thought I had listed all the possible deviations from the standard deep purple, but this year two rose-pink specimens were added to my records – one with an exceptionally broad lip, and the other having the lip fringed as shaggily as the petal of a bogbean flower.

A COUNTRY DIARY 1968

Berkshire: A few years ago, in early spring before our wintering party of short-eared owls had departed, I had the satisfaction of seeing all the five possible species of owl – tawny, barn, long-eared, short-eared and little – during the same day in this neighbourhood. Just after dawn on a recent morning, when the promise of another flaming June day was obvious even if the thermometer on the grass stated that the ground-level air was only six degrees above freezing-point, a similar 'possible' was scored, this time mainly aurally, with regard to British pigeons and doves. The mixture of cooing, purring, grunting and whining from wood-pigeon, turtle-dove, stock-dove and collared dove was expected enough, but the fifth and quite unexpected voice was that of the rock-dove. (Ornithological eyebrows, raised in surprise that this species could have strayed so far from its distant western or northern breeding-caves, may be lowered – I only claim the ancestral voice, not the vocalist.) The singer was a pied bird displaying to three placid and uninterested racing-pigeons on the roof-ridge of the school. The mystery of the attraction of the new premises, causing gatherings of racing birds of up to a score to loiter for days on end, has recently been solved – the broad horizontal fascias, painted an almost sky-blue combined with the vertical white stripes of the window frames, form a pattern much used by pigeon fanciers presumably to make 'home' conspicuous to homing-pigeons.

A COUNTRY DIARY 1969

Loch Rannoch, Perthshire: As in the South, spring was several weeks later than usual up here, and judging by the difference in the stage of development of the lochside flora compared with that during my last stay here two years ago, the lag has persisted. A journey of exactly 500 miles northward has taken me back five or six weeks, for once again I find myself among elder and wild roses in full bloom. But although pale pink and pure white dog roses are plentiful, the equally abundant Northern species, the downy rose, with its denser, bushier habit and its deep pink flowers, is the gayest feature fringing this stretch of the Road to the Isles. I have only been here for a few hours, but already have noted that bird movement has not been delayed by the late season. Already black-throated divers, which move to more extensive waters from the higher lochans where they have nested as soon as their young can fly, are howling and wailing in the middle of the loch, and common sandpipers, oyster-catchers, curlew and whimbrel are feeding or passing along the shore. One disappointment caused by the lateness of the floral season is that the wild raspberries are not yet ripe – but the walk to investigate the chance of fresh, free dessert for tomorrow was fruitful in another way; a presumed curlew came skimming down the hillside towards the road, and just before it settled on the wall of the old graveyard, uttered the teetering call which confirmed my hope that it might be a whimbrel. As soon as it settled, three inquisitive species more at home on such a perch – a stonechat, a meadow pipit and a spotted flycatcher – had settled within a foot or so to inspect the outsize visitor, but apparently without fear or resentment.

A COUNTRY DIARY 1970

Berkshire: In my last Diary (stillborn on account of the strike), I remarked on the sudden abundance of cuckoos which was noted here from the last week of May onwards. For many villagers these were, in fact, the first cuckoos of the year and, for some of the five-year-olds, the first cuckoo calls ever heard, for here in the valley there has been a dearth of this species for several years, although on the Downs nearby no notice-able change has occurred.

I have no explanation to offer for this belated influx. Since cuckoos are highly territorial, it seems unlikely that a considerable number would suddenly decide to change quarters simultaneously some weeks after their first arrival; on the other hand, it seems just as unlikely that a fresh wave of immigrants would arrive so late in the season. But apparently the latter is the more plausible theory, for the appearance of two 'over-shooters' from the South suggests that some northward movement has recently taken place. I had only just put down the telephone after receiving the news that a woodchat shrike had appeared on our Hampshire border, when a caller came to inform me that he had just returned from watching a roller just cross our Surrey boundary. Both, fooled by this flaming June into believing that they were in their Mediterranean haunts, were apparently enjoying a siesta during this morning's search – but I did flush a fair cross-section of Home Counties birdwatchers.

A COUNTRY DIARY 1971

Berkshire/Oxfordshire: 'Little Stints at the Power Station' – to the uninformed passer-by, this message, if overheard as it passed from a car in the road to myself in the garden, must have suggested yet another outbreak of industrial strife – either a go-slow or a reduction in working hours. But the follow-up which (again only to the uninitiated ear) must have sounded like 'and black turns at Dorchester,' would have suggested a wide variety of ominous interpretations. Some 12 hours later, on a very grey early morning, the first gravel-pit pool seemed devoid of waders except for one green sandpiper on a sand spit, and a common sandpiper skimming across to the opposite shore; but eventually movement was spotted, not, as expected, at the water's edge, but against the unhelpful background of a grey brown shoal of silt – with an incipient vegetation of young willows, celery-leaved crowfoot, and docks, to say nothing of rusty oil drums, to hinder clear observation. About half a dozen each of three small waders, ringed plover, dunlin and little ringed plover, were present, but darting around in typical industrious activity were three of a markedly smaller species – our smallest common British wader, the little stint. Across the river at the Oxfordshire pit, the black terns had either departed or were still at roost. But a telephone call from an even earlier visitor to our first site informed me that one had been there before we arrived.

A COUNTRY DIARY 1972

Oxfordshire: If ever in future I waste valuable hours of daylight by staying indoors to watch a tennis final on television I must remember to draw the curtains and screen off the world outside. Last week, during the ladies' singles final, a chance visitor would have had doubts as to my sanity or at least pity for the quality of my eyesight, for it would have appeared that, at a range of some four yards. I was watching the exciting proceedings through powerful binoculars, The true explanation is that a pair of goldfinches kept shuttling to and fro across my line of vision beyond the screen, and as such behaviour usually betrays nest-building activities, I had to determine the focal point of their journeys. However much the grace, determination, and stamina of the human pair might have pleased an advocate of Women's Liberation, the alternative programme which I chose to view would have had the opposite effect, for obviously what was going on was one more example of the unfair status of the female even in the world of goldfinches. The male added colour and vocal encouragement to his mate, and dutifully accompanied her on every journey, but he did not bring back a single morsel of cobweb or moss – although, to his credit, it must be admitted that he sang continuously and flirted his tail in an ecstasy of approval while his wife fashioned the tight little cup right at the apex of the small walnut tree in the paddock.

A COUNTRY DIARY 1973

Oxfordshire: It has always puzzled me that although the blossoms of hawthorn, dogrose and honeysuckle have received ample attention from poets during the past five centuries, one of the outstanding adornments of the English hedgerow, the elder, seems to have received far less attention than it deserves. In the recent glorious sunshine its huge creamy plates of bloom have stolen the scene along miles of roadside hedges where, by comparison, the delicate pink festoons and billows of dogrose have been far less conspicuous. Shakespeare's references are almost entirely derogatory, ranging from 'stinking elder' to sinister connections with murder, and hollowness of heart. But it seems that in the North country the tree was recognised for its fresh midsummer beauty, not, as hereabouts, merely as a promise of a bumper crop of the berries so valued for that excellent winter cordial, mulled elderberry wine. The sound of a tractor-drawn grass mower has just reminded me that at this season, some 60 years ago, sprigs of elder-bloom were tucked in the horses' collars to keep the flies away as the grass was mown. But the clue which suggested that elder was once an honoured plant came from my mother, when as a very small boy I was sent out to gather firewood. Her favourites were a mysterious substance known as what sounded like 'beerax' (for which dead beech twigs seemed to suffice) or the dead twigs of 'poor try'. The latter I soon realised was elder, and I always assumed that both names were Gaelic. Many years later I discovered that, allowing for the Highland change of certain consonants, her 'poor try' was nothing but the Lowland Scots 'boor tree' – the tree eminently suitable for a shady bower.

A COUNTRY DIARY 1974

Oxfordshire: 'Anon it grew dark, and as it grew dark we had the pleasure to see several glow worms.' Thus wrote Pepys about 300 years ago. Whether these luminous beetles still give pleasure to the late night traveller between Epsom and London I do not know, but certainly in my own area nowadays the pleasure is equally thrilling even if only a single insect is encountered. Before the general diminution of many species of once common insects which began somewhere around the early sixties, downland trackways above my former Berkshire home were lit by the fascinating greenish blue pinpoints of light at frequent intervals, and I often brought a specimen home and placed it in a position where we could experience Samuel Pepys's simple pleasure from the bedroom window. (Conservationists might frown on such interference, but such was the abundance in those good old days that invariably, within a day or so, a winged male was found attached to the female, and so the function of the mysterious cold light was fulfilled.) Recently a friend informed me that she had seen one glowing on the grass verge just by our railway station, but somehow the occurrence slipped her mind, and she did not tell me until a week had elapsed. I went straight to the site as soon as it was sufficiently dark, and was disappointed to discover that the grass had been mown. But from beneath one swath of hay the old familiar light shone out brightly. Fearing that the grass would probably be raked up and burnt, I decided to transfer this specimen to safer quarters. On the way home, in spite of the late hour, I decided to give some kindred spirits a treat, and tapped on their window. It says a great deal both for the sort of friends I have and for the fascination of the glow worm, that, although aroused from bed and bath respectively, the silent answer to the query 'Who's there?' – the illumination of my face by the glow worm light – was received with delight.

A COUNTRY DIARY 1975

Ballyconneely, Connemara: On previous visits to this area, always in August or early September, I have noted, from the evidence of gone-to-seed specimens, that orchids of many species are abundant. Now, at last, I have been able to discover them in bloom. But apart from the lesser butterfly in totally unexpected sites – varying from acid bog to hillsides strewn with limestone boulders – I am still not much the wiser as to the identity of many of my finds, beyond deciding that they are either distinct Western Irish varieties of some of the numerous species of marsh orchids. or, more confusing still, hybrids between some of these. But there was no doubt as to the identity of the bird which struck up a lullaby as my tired head touched the pillow on my first night here. It was a corncrake calling from the grass field just beneath my window. I was delighted to hear the monotonous rasping disyllables once again, and gaily started to count the number of calls in one bout. The first sample only reached 54, so I thought I would test a few more to get an average figure. But when the second spell had exceeded 500 I was tired of being commanded to 'Wake, wake', and was quite relieved when the caller paused for breath when the score had reached 632. Apart from the magnificent and tantalising orchids, a familiar enough flower – the yellow flag iris – here presents an unfamiliar picture, for instead of merely edging watercourses it has in many cases completely taken over whole fields.

A COUNTRY DIARY 1976

Oxfordshire: Primroses still abound among the moss in the more open sections of our local forest, being perhaps at their best along the edges of the wide green rides. In the latter open sites cowslips are also at their best, and somewhere between the two – more often among the primroses than near the cowslips, occurs the fairly common hybrid between the two species. As a boy, following local usage, I knew these as oxlips, but soon found myself corrected when in the presence of adult botanists: oxlips, I was solemnly informed, did not grow in Oxfordshire, and were a distinct species of native primula confined to a few areas of East Anglia. But the influence of both parental and pedagogic mentors has waned with the passing years, and to me the charming primrose/cowslip hybrid is once again the oxlip, as I strongly suspect it has been for many centuries. Shakespeare refers to the oxlip at least twice and it seems highly unlikely that he knew of the eastern plant which some botanists now claim is the one true oxlip. One textbook authority even goes so far as to label Shakespeare's flower 'the false oxlip'; another gets over the difficulty less offensively by referring to the hybrid as the common oxlip, leaving plain oxlip for the rarer species. But to me our local plant is the 'bold oxlip' of the mixed bouquet in *The Winter's Tale* – and, of course, the one which grows on the well-known bank 'where the wild thyme blows.'

A COUNTRY DIARY 1977

Oxfordshire: It always puzzles me that although the goldfinch exhibits such fastidious craftsmanship in the construction of its snug little nest, the final masterpiece is often secured to a flimsy and wind-tossed anchorage.

The favoured fork at the tip of a bough of apple or plum is fairly safe, but similar positions on horse chestnuts (in my experience preferred to all other sites when available) often lead to the tossing out of eggs or young, or even the nest itself. The hen which for some time had been gathering moss from my lawn, root-fibres and fine stems from the borders, and cobwebs from my dry-stone wall, finally built just across the lane high up on the outside of my neighbour's laburnum. Following the near-gale which fanned the Jubilee bonfires I found the nest next morning on my lawn some fifteen yards away, and nearby there lay an unbroken egg. Analysis of the still intact structure revealed that all the materials except one could have been gathered from my garden – and the exceptional item is the one which always interests me, for the basic felt-like inner cup is almost invariably composed of vegetable fluff. In this case the woolly down from sallow seeds, from the valley about a quarter of a mile away possibly, had been used, but in season poplars, thistles, dandelions or cornflowers may provide this essential basic material. I have even known the fluff to be gathered from the woolly leaves of mullein and rose campion, and the only variation I have come across was when the emptying of a carpet-sweeper provided the materials for colourful felt.

A COUNTRY DIARY 1978

Oxfordshire: On a recent sunny morning I spent a most rewarding hour or so in florally rich fenland. Among the reeds, rushes and sedges, more particularly on open patches where these were less crowded, two orchids were still in full bloom – the graceful marsh helleborine and the bright purple spikes of the fen fragrant orchis – the latter a much more robust and more pleasantly scented form of the common species of chalk downland. Two insectivorous plants – butterwort and bladderwort – were also found, but the cushions of sphagnum, on which sundew used to grow, failed to provide the third possible species, probably because the only specimens of this moss discovered were too well shaded by the dominant reeds. Apart from the flowers, which included many others only to he found in such habitats, two items of fauna in fact provided the highlights of the visit. To see scarlet tiger moths – no less than seven on a short transit of one patch – was an understandable thrill, for this spectacular species is decidedly local in its distribution; but the fact is that the sight of a large grass snake basking in the sun, and then the disappearing tail of another, were for me occurrences of almost equal rarity, for although I regularly visit old woodland haunts where once these reptiles abounded, during the seven years since my return here I have so far seen none. No, I have not been on one of my usual trips to my favourite fenland patch in Norfolk Breckland; only in fact to a site within a few miles of Oxford city itself.

A COUNTRY DIARY 1979

Oxfordshire: Although at least one pair of buzzards inhabits our large patch of ancient woodland, one rarely sees them outside the confines of the forest. Although I visit the latter at least weekly, this year I have so far encountered them once only – a pair together in mid-February. But game-keepers daily patrolling the area report much more frequent sight-ings and one can only conclude that, unlike their more conspicuous counterparts in moorland and mountain districts, they can obtain food, particularly rabbits, without extensive foraging flights and, once gorged, retire to digest their meal in the treetops where they remain secreted for the rest of the day. But occasionally, in suitable weather conditions when gliding and soaring practice may be enjoyed in uprising thermal currents, buzzards may leave their secret haunts and perform their leisurely manoeuvres over our little town itself. But in nine years' residence I have only witnessed this thrice – single birds on two occasions, but, a few years ago when successful breeding was reported by the head-keeper (and this in itself, on an estate where pheasant-rearing and shooting are major activ-ities, is a heartening fact), the whole family of four, on one hot evening in late summer, ventured out to disport themselves high over the rooftops. So when, on a bright and cloudless afternoon a few days ago, I spotted a large predator high overhead, I straightway assumed it was a buzzard, until, even without the aid of binoculars, I realised that it was not of the right shape – its wings were too pointed and its tail too long, and in my pocket-book I noted 'about size of buzzard, but falcon-like.' The mystery might never have been solved but for sheer luck, for the bird reappeared above my house on the following afternoon. This time binoc-ulars were available, and it was discernible that, although when gliding into the wind its wings were markedly falcon-like, on the opposite tack the tips of the primaries were 'fingered' and the bird assumed a shape which I recognised – that of a goshawk. My lingering doubt as to identity was resolved by discovering, on consulting *Birds of Prey in the Field*, that 'When gliding into headwind, wings may look quite pointed, and goshawk may then resemble large falcon.'

A COUNTRY DIARY 1980

Oxfordshire: A few days ago I feared that, after an absence of several years, a mole had found its way into my garden from the surrounding fields, for as I examined the progress of my runner beans, the soil between the rows began to move at one spot, and soon a little mound was forming on the surface. From the intermittent nature of the eruption – short spells of great activity interspersed with long pauses – I concluded that only a mole could be capable of such energetic earth-moving, but I was both relieved and puzzled at what finally broke through the loosened soil – not the pink nose of a mole, but the broad amber-eyed head of a large toad. After watching its efforts to extricate itself for some time, I concluded that its body must have been too broad to follow its head upwards, and accordingly I loosened the restraining crust with my knife, and a full-grown female toad emerged. A few weeks previously the ground for the bean-row had been deeply trenched and manured with mushroom-compost, and, of course, the site had been trodden firm before the beans were planted out. Since a toad would be incapable of burrowing down into such firm soil, one can only conclude that it was already underground before the beans were planted out, and the most plausible explanation would seem to be that it had chosen my stack of manure (which had been deposited at the site for some weeks) as a damp and warm retreat, and had inadvertently been buried with a forkful of this material.

A COUNTRY DIARY 1981

Loch Rannoch: At this time of year this lovely loch is singularly devoid of aquatic bird life, and until a few minutes ago I had seen none afloat apart from common and black-headed gulls, an oystercatcher swimming well offshore from its nesting-site, a single mallard, and, usually twice daily, a red-throated diver. The dearth is not peculiar to my particular location, but general. I had just remarked that things would liven up later when the mergansers brought their broods down from the burns, and the divers with their offspring came down from the high lochans where they nest, when I spotted in mid-loch what I at first took to be canoes with crews of two and eight respectively. The apparitions turned out to be two parties of geese, one of two greylags with four goslings strung closely together between them, followed by a party of seven Canadas accompanied by a nondescript pale greyish goose which was probably a hybrid. Whether or not these greylags are genuine wild birds or, like the Canadas, the feral descendants of deliberately introduced birds, is an unanswerable question, but from the size of the youngsters, they had hatched somewhere locally. There are, alas, no dippers to entertain us with their sub-aquatic activities, and cheerful warblings, for the semi-submerged boulders just beneath the window which used to be much favoured are now completely under water, and the sandy strand has likewise disappeared. The depth of the loch, is controlled by 'the hydro-electric', and unfortunately I gather that the level is raised just as the oystercatchers are nesting between the shore-line boulders. Some are now making second attempts on higher ground, and the common sandpipers, which abound all along the shore, tend in any case to nest well above the waterline. I have just flushed one from its nest in a birch wood over a hundred yards from the loch.

A COUNTRY DIARY 1982

Oxfordshire: A correspondent who lives in a village below White Horse Hill has on his property some tall old maples, of various species, some of which seem to have been badly affected by the extreme climatic conditions of last winter. Accordingly, early on the morning of May 15, he used his binoculars to examine the topmost twigs. Whether or not he discovered any signs of arboreal life he did not say, for the purport of his message was to tell me that he had found that he had focused on a strikingly coloured strange bird basking in the early sunshine. It was about the size of a starling, and of a brilliant yellow with black wings and tail, and on consulting his bird-book the beneficiary of this supreme example of serendipity decided that it was a veritable golden oriole. Although this species is a rare visitor to either Oxfordshire or Berkshire (there are only about a dozen authenticated records for the last hundred years or more), apart from the fact that the observer had excellent views of a bird which usually proclaims its presence by its lovely fluting call and remains hidden in a leafy tree-top, a chance piece of information from the Bird Observatory on Portland Bill has confirmed my belief that the identification was correct. At this favoured staging-post for migrants a golden oriole appeared on May 10, and stayed until May 14, on which date it was joined by a second specimen, so that it seems that these spectacular birds are on their way to their breeding-grounds, whether to the secret site in the eastern counties where there is a small colony, or whether they have drifted off-course en route for continental sites.

A COUNTRY DIARY 1983

Oxfordshire: Just as *Nasturtium*, which was originally the generic name for our native water-cress species, has now been firmly attached to the totally unrelated *Tropaeolum*, so the geranium family suffers from confusion in nomenclature. Thus the popular bedding 'geranium' belongs to the closely-related genus *Pelargonium*, a name now reserved by gardeners for a greenhouse species of the same group. The two generic names refer to the beak-like formation of the seed-capsules, referring to the crane in the case of the geranium, and the stork in pelargonium. But, to confuse matters further, the storksbill name in vernacular usage, refers to yet another genus, the *Erodiums*, ferny-leaved and pink-flowered mat-formers on sandy turf. But of the true geraniums or cranesbills we have an abundance of native species, some mere weeds, such as the dovesfoot, cut-leaved and small-flowered cranesbills, while others, however common in suitable habitats, can be truly splendid. The humblest of these, herb Robert, needs dryish conditions, such as an old wall, a quarry face, or even an uprooted tree-stump, to produce its most colourful effect – the contrast between crimson-tinted stems and foliage and pink flowers. Recently I came across such colourful cushions high above the normal vegetation-line on otherwise sterile shingle on Chesil Bank. But although I have been duly impressed by mounds of the bloody cranesbill on the limestone pavements of The Burren, and the mauve wood cranesbill contrasting with neighbouring globe-flowers on the shores of Highland lochs, I still maintain that our local species, the meadow cranesbill, is the queen of the family. Some of our minor roads are now lined with the large blue flowers above the deeply cut foliage, but, living up to their name, the finest local specimens come from an extensive colony in a narrow strip of meadow along the Evenlode, regularly flooded in winter. Here, for good measure, they are interspersed with the taller creamy blooms of meadow-sweet.

A COUNTRY DIARY 1984

Oxfordshire: As a change from my periodic lamentations over the virtual disappearance locally of species of wildlife, I can report with great pleasure that, contrary to my observations during the past 14 years, bats are not in this category of near extinction. Up to about ten years ago I did have long-eared bats in my garden shed, but since then I had seen none around the house until one warm night this June – and then there were only two. But a few days ago a local resident informed me that his house was 'infested ' with bats, and he had contacted the Rural District Council's pest officer with a view to their destruction. This request might have been complied with at one time. But thanks to recent legislation which gives all species of bats complete protection, the response from the authorities was 'On no account interfere with them, and inform the local office of the Nature Conservancy Council of their presence.' This has been duly done, and I expect to join the specialist in his investigation of the colony shortly. But in the meantime I have visited the site, and from around 9 pm onwards witnessed them dropping out from a small hole above a lintel, and all winging their way to nearby parkland.

A COUNTRY DIARY 1985

Oxfordshire: My reference in last week's Diary to the careless spraying of the edges of the brook with selective weedkiller intended to kill all herbage except grasses in the meadows alongside, has aroused the question as to whether the resulting purity of the crop – hay in this case – pays for the considerable expenditure both on chemicals and labour involved. Certainly in the case of weeds poisonous to stock, such as ragwort, the procedure would be justifiable. But in the absence of such pest species the so-called 'weeds' – such as dandelion, daisies, knapweed, yarrow and plantain – are in fact desirable constituents of pastures and hayfields. Research has shown that these and many other wild natives in grass are rich in minerals essential in a balanced diet for stock. Just after posting last week's piece I came across a nice comment on the problem from the beasts concerned. I happened to walk through a former playing field, now disused and being allowed to 'tumble down to grass,' on to which cattle and sheep had been put a day or two earlier. I was at first surprised that little impression seemed to have been made on the herbage, now about nine inches high; but then I realised that not a single bloom of the former abundant dandelion blossom was to be seen, and that the flowers and/or foliage of these plants, with those of ribwort plantain, yarrow and cats-ear, had been gnawed down to ground level, while the grass itself was less heavily grazed.

A COUNTRY DIARY 1986

Oxfordshire: A visitor to my garden, always welcome because of his adherence to the now almost obsolete dialect which was general in my boyhood, inquired as to the correct name of 'they blue flowers as we 'ad always used to call pennies.' But for the latter clue, I should have been puzzled, for the only blue flowers in sight were those of forget-me-nots. I then realised that he was using 'blue' to describe the pinkish-mauve blooms of honesty (*Lunaria annua*), and this usage of the word to embrace a wide spectrum of colours also occurs in the vernacular names of some of our wild flowers. Thus the early purple orchid, although Shakespeare in a neighbouring county knew it as 'long purples', is still known locally as 'blue butcher' – with an alternative, 'Bloody Butcher', equating blue with sanguine red, by which analogy we can all claim to be blue-blooded. Blue also occurs in the West Country name blue bottles for the knapweed, which has reddish-purple blossoms. One is tempted by these long-established examples to wonder whether the use of the word blue to signify either depression or pornography harks back to this looser usage of the term; certainly a sullen shade of dull purple, rather than the splendour of an open sky or the blooms of gentian, seems more appropriate, and springs to mind when I hear it mentioned in such connections.

PS: It came as a surprise to me to read in my last Country Diary (May 14) that the fox was 'furiously feeding' on the lambs' tails; what I wrote merely stated that it was 'very actively engaged in finding food.'

A COUNTRY DIARY 1987

Oxfordshire: Two regular indicators of the turn of the year have appeared on time. The first was the general blooming of the first spikes of rose-bay willowherb on the first day of July. Then came the first signs of the return 'autumn' migration of summer migrants: the usual pioneers in the form of common sandpipers, four of which were at the reservoirs near Oxford on July 11. But a few nights ago I witnessed an unusual movement of birds for which I can offer no explanation. At 9.30 pm when dusk fell early under a cloudy sky – I had already seen four hedgehogs out and about and bats were on the wing – I was surprised to see a party of 32 black-headed gulls flying steadily on a westerly course. As only silhouettes were observable in the fading light, I was unable to determine whether they were adults or non-breeding immatures. This species has bred successfully on an islet in a gravel-pit pool about 12 miles away, but from the line of flight of these nocturnal travellers this source seems unlikely. In a few weeks' time the passage of gulls over my house will be a daily occurrence continuing throughout autumn and winter; but the lesser black-backs, black-headed, and herring gulls commute on a roughly south-north passage in the morning, reversed on the return journey, usually well before dusk. This movement is explicable: they roost on the reservoirs and gravel-pit pools, and commute to forage on refuse dumps, the latest of which is only a few miles north of my house.

A COUNTRY DIARY 1988

Oxfordshire: The seed-leaves of dicotyledons are often totally unlike the mature leaves which follow: familiar examples are those of the lime-tree and morning glory (*Ipomoea*), whose first pairs of leaves resemble those of a cut-leaved maple, rather than the heart-shaped foliage of the adult stage. Therefore when some unfamiliar seedlings appeared this spring beneath my globe-flowers (*Trollius*), despite the fact that the roundish leaves did not resemble those of the presumed parent above, I hopefully pricked out a few, and grew them on. They are now large enough for identification, and my initial assumption has been proved incorrect, for what I now have is a box of sturdy plants of marsh marigolds – locally known either as king-cups or water-bubbles. This is yet one more species to be added to my list of marsh plants almost certainly introduced in dressings of sedge-peat from Somerset, for in the same herbaceous border, where mounds of this material are used for winter protection of subjects such as paeonies, I have recorded yellow flag iris, creeping jenny, water chickweed, celery-leaved crowfoot and meadow-sweet, all of which have been grown on to the flowering stage. In the nearby rose bed, similarly treated, a clump of sedge has grown, and from its subsequent flowers is undoubtedly the long-bracted sedge (*Carex extensa*); this species, according to my flora, is a plant of grassy salt-marshes, but since it does not occur locally, is probably yet another peat-borne immigrant. But some of the welcome 'adventives' (a better term than mere 'weeds') in my garden, also recognised as seedlings and allowed to remain, are of local origin. Three which occur annually are caper spurge, night-flowering catchfly, and nettle-leaved bellflower, none of which is now common in the wild. The last of these established itself in a clump of hosta, and now, nicely complemented by the elegant pale mauve blooms of the hosta which surround it, flaunts a tall spire of about sixty purplish-blue bells.

A COUNTRY DIARY 1989

Kenfig, Glamorgan: Within three hours of leaving home at 5 am (BST), I found myself in the floral paradise of this nature reserve – a maze of old sand-dunes interspersed with fenny hollows – 'dune slacks.' Although the main object of the trip was to find the rare and elusive fen orchid, I should have been satisfied if, as after several hours of searching seemed likely, it had not been achieved, for the sheer wealth of other flora would have been worthwhile. The outstanding species were the two marsh orchids – the early and the southern, and although I am familiar with these in a few local sites on my home ground, these, in species prone to much regional variation, were outstandingly different. The southern marsh were robust specimens with bright purple or occasionally pinker columnar flower-spikes up to six inches high, whilst the early marsh had conical flower-spikes of a brick-red hue. As a result of the drought, it was odd to see such semi-aquatic species as bog pimpernel, marsh helleborine orchids, yellow loosestrife, lesser spearwort, tubular water-dropwort and lesser water-plantain flourishing in apparently dry turf; and it was here eventually, having spent hours in investigating wetter sites, that I found the first specimen of the tiny green orchid – and once spotted, 14 others were soon added. A single bee orchid, mats of the white-flowered burnet rose, and clumps of the handsome blue spikes of viper's bugloss adorned the drier and higher mounds, whilst all round the grass-stems were festooned with the parchment-like cocoons of the six-spot burnet moth, hundreds of which had emerged and were on the wing. But the outstanding butterfly was the dark green fritillary, of which I counted over a score, recalling the days when it abounded on my home-ground, but no longer does so. To end a perfect day we came home through the Gloucestershire Cotswolds, where I brought my score of British orchids up to 40, with my first ever red helleborines – well protected by a wire fence, but visible at very close range. But perhaps the most rewarding aspect of this memorable day was that my companion and instigator of the expedition was a former pupil whose interests I aroused by pre-school trips to a local sewage-farm in search of waders.

A COUNTRY DIARY 1990

Oxfordshire: In contrast with the highly successful orchid foray which I reported last week, a visit to a site in my local woodland has proved depressing. Here, in damp grass bordering numerous Wychwood streams, at this season one may find a spectacular mixture of orchids in bloom – twayblades, southern marsh orchid, spotted orchid, and hybrids between the latter two which excel their parents in both size and colour, followed later by pyramidal orchids on the drier slopes. But on a recent visit to one of the best colonies where there had been promise of a good show a few weeks ago, I could not find a single flowering specimen of any of the species, and the reason was all too evident. A search revealed the basal leaves of the plants. particularly noticeable in the case of the twayblades, whose two eponymous leaves were still intact, but in every instance the flower-stem had been nipped off – and slots of deer on the muddy edges of the stream provided strong circumstantial evidence as to the culprits, a conclusion further supported by the fact that no such depredations occurred in the forest in the good old days when deer were strictly confined to the adjacent park. A similar fate to that of the orchids has prevented the once plentiful stinking hellebore, which used to grow in bushy colonies of scores on stony banks, from regenerating, and since in this case also only the lower heads are nipped off, deer are the suspects, for although no slots provide a clue, I have found their droppings nearby. But my despondency was slightly alleviated, at a point by the stream well away from the ravaged main colony, by the discovery of a patch of about 20 of the southern marsh in full bloom.

A COUNTRY DIARY 1991

Oxfordshire: I thought I should have to confine my observations to garden subjects this week, as I am not yet very mobile, so I began periodic counts of the butterflies on the buddleias. By far the most abundant species has been the peacock: my maximum count has been 41 peacocks, one each of red admiral, small tortoiseshell and brimstone, and all too many large whites. But the sight of a single willow warbler turned my thoughts to the fact that summer migrants would now be dispersing and that normally I would be visiting Farmoor reservoirs in the hope of spotting waders and passerines on passage. As disabled anglers are allowed to drive around the pools, I asked by telephone if the same concession could be granted to a bird-watcher, and accordingly a few hours later found myself being driven slowly, with frequent stops, around the perimeter. My hunch as to passage in progress proved correct, and although the occasional rarity may provide a thrill, I am content when I see the birds which I expect to see at this season, and this duly happened. The most abundant species, of which we must have flushed hundreds from the roads on our circuit, was the yellow wagtail, with juveniles predominating. The only wader encountered was the one expected – the common sand-piper – of which we flushed ten or perhaps a dozen, some singly and some in threes or fours, from the water's edge. Then a larger and more erect bird than a wagtail appeared on the wall, and as it flew, revealing its white rump, proved to be another expected species – the wheatear, which was joined by another as it bounced away. Apart from these three passage birds, the only other summer visitors, probably local breeders, seen, were a small party of sand martins and a few swallows and house martins.

Finally, may I proffer a sincere thank you to the numerous well-wishers who have written to me.

A COUNTRY DIARY 1992

Oxfordshire: My conclusion that the pair of long-tailed tits which regularly foraged along the framework of my large bay window, presumably gathering small insects or spiders, had a nestful of young somewhere nearby, has been strengthened by the appearance of nine youngsters having difficulty in balancing themselves, with tail-upward postures on the overhead wires, whilst the two parents were busy exploring the foliage of the greengage below. But even more pleasing than this sight was a sound from a hedge just up the lane – the purring of a turtledove, once one of the common accompaniments of lazy summery weather. Last year my only local record was of one which called for a week from the same hedge, but, presumably failing to attract a mate, it moved on.

There is no doubt that the organised slaughter of these birds by the tens of thousands as they enter southern Europe from African winter quarters has led to the much diminished number which now reach the British Isles. As Solomon said: 'The time of the singing of birds is come, and the voice of the turtle is heard in our land,' but for how long will this be true in the case of this harmless little dove? My two weeping buddleias flanking my entrance gates scent the air with a distinctly honey-like aroma – yet they seem to fail to attract bees or butterflies to the hundreds of yard-long mauve tassels. It seems that this species (*B. alternfolia*), unlike its commoner relative, the butterfly bush, flowers a few weeks too early for the emergence of some of our larger and most colourful butterflies. But even though the buddleias were available, my first painted lady of the year chose the humbler, but spicily aromatic flowers of sweet rocket or dame's violet. This, June 10, is my earliest-ever record for this species, which normally I expect joining the peacocks and red admirals on the buddleias in August. It is now pretty well established that the painted lady is a migrant from the Mediterranean region, moving northward in series of halts and hops, and breeding as it goes. Thus my most spectacular ever record of this species was high in the hills above Loch Ettrick, when seven in mint condition were on a patch of thistles in August, but their grand-parent may have hatched in north Africa.

A COUNTRY DIARY 1993

Oxfordshire: A resident recently brought me a strange plant which had appeared in her garden. It had been identified as hop, but I immediately recognised it as white bryony, because the enquirer had dug up the complete plant, and its tap-root could have been mistaken for a fair-sized parsnip. The sight of the latter brought back memories from about 60 years ago, when I learned that this plant was only the third British native which was still being used medicinally, although in a veterinary rather than a human context. The occasion was memorable because of the name given to this plant. I was passing a hunting-stable, and looked in for a word with the groom, who was preparing a mash for his horses. Producing a knife, he went to the wall where what looked like a shrivelled parsnip was hanging, and preceeded to pare off slivers which he mixed with the mash. 'What's that?' I asked and he replied, 'Mandrake, the best physic as there is for 'osses.' This name led me to wonder whether the plant which Shakespeare knew by this name ('The insane root which takes the reason prisoner') was this common hedgerow native, and not the true mandragora from more southerly regions which does not flourish in our climate. On consulting my *Extra Pharmocopeia*, I was delighted to find white bryony listed as 'English or False Mandrake' a tincture of which was once recommended as a remedy for coughs and pleurisy. A feature of this plant is the speed with which the young shoots emerge in spring – six inches in 24 hours. This flying start is doubtless due to the impetus provided by the reserve of food stored in the outsize tap-root, which, according to early herbalists, might be as big as a one-year-old child and weigh 'Halfe an hundred waight'. Although this bryony is the only British member of the cucumber and marrow family, the other sharer of the name, the black bryony, is our only member of the yam family, and also shares the large underground food-store and has a similar rapid emergence in spring.

A COUNTRY DIARY 1994

Oxfordshire: In 1932 I gave my brother, two years my senior, *The Ornithologists' Field Book*. The preliminary list of British birds was duly ticked off as his records increased, but the main part of the book, lined blank pages, was untouched for the following 12 years. Ian, a telegraphist, had joined the London Fire Service at the outbreak of war, but getting bored during the period before the blitz, managed to resign and join the RAF. From then on his lips were sealed; we assumed that he was connected with a hush-hush service involving usually air force uniforms but sometimes khaki with an anchor emblem on the shoulder – hints of what we came to know as Combined Ops. I took possession of his bird diary after his death a few years ago, and found that he had written it up almost daily since his arrival in Normandy on June 7. The entries were terse, such as 'good dry landing – shot at by E-boat on way, and a sniper on landing. Bout of digging our lovely dugout. Noisy night.' But in the early days there was no mention of birds and it was only in later conversations I learned that he had flushed a peregrine on the final ascent of a cliff, and though tempted to look for the nest, continued his hurried upward journey. No hints as to the activities of his group, but when he was demobbed all came out – his was a very secret unit with a wagon containing the newly invented radar apparatus. He loved telling of how they were instructed to let no one in, not even the C-in-C, without written authorisation. Later Ian seemed to pay greater attention to birds, and was very impressed by a noisy night of Manx shearwater calls, with which he had become familiar on a joint visit to the Pembroke island of Skokholm. There were references to passages of migrants like yellow wagtails, wheatears, and redstarts. Ian returned home unscathed except for a broken wrist from a champagne-induced tumble from a lorry. His next bird note of interest was of black redstarts nesting high up on Paddington Station.

12

COUNTRY DIARIES – AUTUMN

A COUNTRY DIARY 1964

Berkshire: Although the bulk of the swallow and martin population departed some weeks ago, stragglers may still be seen. Indeed some house-martins could not have made their first flights until this month, for on the last day of September I discovered one nest where youngsters were still being fed. A touch of urgency attended this feeding, for not only the two parents, but also at least two other martins were busy carrying food to the same nest. Since martins are not nocturnal migrants, I have often wondered what happens to birds seen disappearing to the SSW in the late afternoon. On October 9, having seen three house-martins travelling in this direction at about 4 p.m. (GMT), I was surprised to hear flight calls again almost two hours later. But these birds did not pass on; two descended abruptly and began fluttering round the eaves of a tall building exactly in the manner of birds prospecting for a nesting-site. I feel sure that if any old martin's nest had been available, it would have been occupied for a night's lodging. Early next morning, just as the ground was beginning to whiten with the hoar frost which had not been present at dawn, I discovered the two birds huddled together on a narrow ledge beneath the eaves. One flew at my approach, but the other was so moribund that I was able to pick it up. After an hour in a dark box behind the stove, it began to announce its recovery by twittering and fluttering, and soon it had joined its fellow-traveller in the early sunshine.

A COUNTRY DIARY 1965

Berkshire: Chiffchaffs are still plentiful in and around my garden, but it is noticeable that the frequent bursts of song are now followed by that peculiar subdued creaking which invariably accompanies the waning of breeding activity in early summer. Of the other summer visitors both house-martins and swallows are still present in small numbers; some of the former are still feeding late broods, and on the last day of September four newly flown swallows, looking bedraggled and almost moribund (except when food arrived) were experiencing their first contact with the British open air. They were perched in what would normally have been a sheltered site, on some telegraph wires overhung by a poplar, but the saturated umbrella had begun to leak, and the unfortunate fledglings were receiving a baptism more concentrated than they would have had beneath the open sky. But most other summer visitors have gone, and I have just received news of one which was well on its way to Africa just about three weeks ago. This was a spotted flycatcher which was ringed in my garden on September 5, and was 'recovered' dead near Bilbao, Spain, on September 20. I fear that 'recovery' here is a euphemism for a violent end from gunshot, traps, nets or birdlime; if I could brief my birds before their southward departure, they would be instructed to steer clear of this area, for two other of 'my' birds, a whitethroat and a jacksnipe have been the victims of similar recoveries 'near Bilbao'.

A COUNTRY DIARY 1966

Berkshire: On several sunny afternoons recently atmospheric conditions have seemed ideal for a fall of gossamer, but apart from the occasional glint of a floating thread high up among the swallows and fly-catching starlings, and the drifting down of the cottony clot as the migrant parachutist came to earth, there has been no spectacular appearance of this phenomenon. Nevertheless, the foggy early mornings have brought into prominence the activities of more earth-bound spiders, so much so that the moisture-laden webs become the most striking feature of the scenery. Whether the sheet-webs, dry and invisible, had been present on my patch of lily-of-the-valley before the onset of the fog I do not know; but at dawn the bed of fading foliage had been transformed by a random arrangement of horizontal sheets of muslin-like web. On closer examination these somewhat sagging sheets are seen to be the bases of purse-like structures, and then the total pattern is quite reminiscent of a microscopic section of cellular tissue. Between the stems of a row of hollyhocks was an even more striking display, for in addition to the tiers of sheet-webs just above ground-level almost every stem at higher levels was the support of the garden spider's vertical orb-web. Whereas the webs of the sheet-building spider appear to be of gauzy felt, these orb-webs are truly woven. But it is a bewildering exercise, particularly before breakfast, to follow the course of the woof to prove that it proceeds spirally, and that the finished pattern is not, as it appears, a series of concentric polygons.

A COUNTRY DIARY 1967

Berkshire: The accepted ornithological usage of 'gull' instead of 'sea-gull,' whether it was adopted merely for brevity or in recognition of the fact that some fresh-water species of this group exist, is becoming more and more appropriate for the lesser black-backed gull, which in the not very distant past was a truly marine bird. Even before the end of July small parties were regularly passing over my garden towards the rubbish dump in the morning, and towards some thirty-mile-distant reservoirs in the evening. During my absence about a month ago, an observer noted that a flock of some two hundred was feeding at the dump. I was passing this site in the late afternoon a few days ago, when a continuous stream was noted leaving the pit and moving in the roostward direction. Having estimated that over two hundred had passed over, and that judging from the cloud circling above the pool many more were preparing to follow, I moved to a strategic position from which I felt sure I should get a view of the departing flock as it appeared against the sky-line; this was not only for the purpose of making a count, but also for the pleasure of watching the precise goose-like formations which are usually assumed before big flights. But no birds reappeared, and I realised that it was too early for the roosting-flight. Luckily the flock had settled on a roadside field which I had to pass on the way home – and the black acres of burnt straw, doubtless containing instant ready-roasted gull-supper cereal, made a conveniently barren background for an accurate count. Apart from two or three black-headed gulls and countless lapwings (literally so, because they were immobile and matched the charred background), there were no fewer than 760 lesser black-backs present.

A COUNTRY DIARY 1968

Berkshire: If the sludge from our local sewage disposal works had, during the ten years of the plant's existence, been dumped to form a deep surface stratum, some future investigator would find a rich source for bird fossils. But the puzzling feature for the future palaeo-ornithologist would be the circumstances in which obvious land birds, mainly seed-eaters, had become embedded in organic mud. Just over four years ago I wrote of the discovery of the corpses of seventy-three house sparrows, together with single specimens of skylark, blackbird and partridge, from the semi-liquid sludge against the smooth, vertical wall of the bed. Since then I have kept the site under regular watch, and until recently have found no cause for concern. But a few days ago a worker from the site brought me a ring from one 'my' greenfinches which had made the fatal error of landing on liquid which appeared to be solid, and therefore I have just made a careful survey. The corpses this time were all of one species – greenfinches; but the total hooked out – nineteen – only represents the number which managed to flounder to the edge, there to succumb slowly from exhaustion in trying to scale the bounding six inches of wall; at least as many slight bumps on the otherwise level surface mark the graves of those immobilised on first impact with the deceptive landing ground. On each of these known occasions it looks as if the concerted settling of a flock, rather than of individuals at intervals, would explain the numbers involved. The attraction of apparently barren mud to seed-eaters at first seems puzzling. But judging from the lush growth of seedlings on earlier deposits, now dried out, a plentiful food supply is available – tomato seeds.

A COUNTRY DIARY 1969

Rannoch, Perthshire With the abundance of decaying timber – mainly birch – in my immediate neighbourhood, it is not surprising to find that woodpeckers also abound. These, with one interesting exception, have all been of the species which I prefer to call the pied woodpecker, although generally it is known by the inaccurate epithet of great spotted. While watching some of these a few days ago – two on a telegraph post, one on a stone wall, and a fourth on the chimney of the house itself – I spotted a fifth which was truly both great and spotted, for it was a juvenile green woodpecker. Since then I have seen it (or another) on the wall of the graveyard just down the road. The point of interest here is that the green woodpecker in Britain is mainly confined to England and Wales, although of late years there has been a gradual northward spread which has taken it into the Lowlands. Another southerner which has invaded the Highlands in force this year is that splendid butterfly, the painted lady. At 1,300 feet on the shore of Loch Ericht on a recent bright, but decidedly breezy day, I counted at least forty along less than a quarter of a mile of trackway, and at over 2,000 feet on the return journey seven were around one small patch of thistles. The thistles which were the attraction at both sites, incidentally, were of the species which is the obvious heraldic thistle of Scotland – the spear thistle. The so-called Scotch thistle, a much less aggressive cottony alien, was almost certainly not available as symbol at the time of the founding of Scotland's premier order of knighthood.

A COUNTRY DIARY 1970

Oxfordshire: The gravel-pit sandspit, although a very miniature feature compared with the vast acreage of water into which it intrudes, is still proving remarkably attractive to passage waders and winter visitors of the same fascinating family. In the latter category is a flock of 60 or 70 golden plover, parties of which periodically leave the surrounding stubbles for an energetic splashing session in the shallows, quite frequently getting out of their depth and demonstrating their swimming ability. But the star turn of the year so far was a great rarity for this area: an avocet which stayed on the spit for several hours on the morning of October 10. Omitting the unpleasant record of six killed at one shot while swimming at Sonning in 1794 (a border-line county record in any case) this is only the second record of this bird in Oxfordshire. The local carpenter (a most reliable ornithologist) who spotted this rarity was thrilled when the bird obligingly went through its repertory of feeding behaviour – ploughing a straight furrow' as it dashed through the water with its extended beak immersed, and 'scything' the surface with a rapid side-to-side action of its upturned bill as it skimmed the surface for whatever delicacies it had disturbed. This was luck indeed for one seeing this handsome bird for the first time; when I saw it a little later it was apparently replete and fairly static – but nevertheless a delight to watch once again.

A COUNTRY DIARY 1971

Oxfordshire: Some years ago, from Berkshire, I wrote about bird casualties at a local sewage-disposal plant – the victims, immobilised by settling in deceptively solid-looking sludge, dying a slow death from exhaustion after fruitless efforts to get a claw-hold on the few inches of perpendicular smooth wall which barred their way to freedom. Early in the morning a few days ago, while bird-nesting in the cypresses fringing my neighbour's swimming-pool I came across another example of unintentional trapping and slow slaughter of wildlife. A wake moving across the pool attracted my attention, since the presence of a water-vole here, some hundred feet above the Evenlode Valley, seemed unlikely. The swimmer turned out to be a large female hedgehog, puffing out water in the last stages of exhaustion. Rescue was simple, since from time to time she reached the opposite wall at which vain attempts to climb the mere two inches of smooth metal were made, and an hour later she had disappeared from the long grass in which I had placed her. But two decomposing carcases in corners of the pool indicated that this incident was by no means unusual. Since such pools are becoming increasingly popular adjuncts of modern residences, this pitfall aspect should be borne in mind by all owners. My neighbour is planning a ramp or ramps which will facilitate escape.

A COUNTRY DIARY 1972

Oxfordshire: Recently I renewed acquaintance with an octogenarian lady who had been my nearest neighbour, about half a mile away when I was a boy. Naturally we recalled events of half a century ago, and since we had then both been denizens of the ancient Forest of Wychwood, we somehow drifted on to the subject of poachers and gamekeepers, but in no time found ourselves at the Battle of Alma almost precisely 118 years ago. The links in the chain were as follows: Her father-to-be, a Berkshire lad of 18, was returning from work with his rush basket on his shoulders when he was stopped by a gamekeeper who demanded to see the contents of his bag; since it contained only the usual and lawful firewood, the youth refused, and a fight ensued. The gamekeeper had the worst of it, and thinking that the prostrate figure was dead, the youth set out to walk to Winchester, where he took the Queen's shilling. Nothing more was heard of him until he returned from service in both the Crimean War and the Indian Mutiny – and the first person with whom he had a drink in calling at the local inn on his way home was the keeper. But the fascination of this link with the past for me was that after the Battle of Alma, Henry Ostridge and his mates, of the First Battalion of the Royal Scots, composed a poem in the true broadsheet tradition to commemorate their victory, and after almost 80 years of oral transmission I heard the whole of the 17 quatrains without hesitation. Only one point remains obscure – what was the war cry, rendered as 'fogabolyur' which came from 'The Sons of France at Alma'?

A COUNTRY DIARY 1973

Oxfordshire: Recently a late night glance from the kitchen window aroused my interest, for the pulsating red glow on the northern horizon suggested an out-of-season display of the northern lights; but on opening the back door both nose and ears soon corrected this explanation. For not only was the pungent scent of burning vegetation heavy on the air, but also the miniature crackling explosions indicated that green wood as well as dry straw was being incinerated. In spite of much publicised assurances that this year farmers would follow an approved code of practice with regard to the post-harvest disposal of straw, damage this year has been worse than ever before. Mile after mile of hedgerows in this vicinity are now scorched brown, and not only the usual components of local field hedges – hawthorn, blackthorn, bramble, briar, hazel, dogwood, spindle, field maple, and buckthorn – have been destroyed but also sizeable trees of elm, oak, holly and ash, spared by considerate hedgers of the old school, are now scorched and shrivelled ruins. It seems ironic that both the panic about Dutch elm disease and the slogan ' Plant a Tree in 73' should be answered by this wholesale destruction for short term economic gain. The ploughing of a narrow fire break at an approved distance around the headlands has proved to be quite useless, as in the current bone-dry conditions flames leap this barrier with ease. Would it entail much extra labour, with modern mechanical aids, to rake up the straw around the boundaries to a really safe distance away from the hedgerows?

A COUNTRY DIARY 1974

Oxfordshire: From last Sunday onward, the middle Sunday of each month until March is the date appointed for the counting of wildfowl on waters throughout the British Isles, and in England at least there can be few sizeable stretches of fresh water, with a fair sample of salt water included, which will escape the surveillance of devoted observers. Although no longer actively concerned in this thorough national census, I still associate the opening of this season not so much with duck, as it is too early yet for the main winter influx, as with the odds and ends of migratory and passage birds which may be encountered on the September count. Therefore, on the recent appropriate date, I felt the urge to visit old sites and possibly encounter my younger successors. A heavy drizzle and a completely overcast sky almost deterred me from setting out, but as it happened these very conditions were ideal for causing a 'fall' of birds which, in brighter conditions, would almost certainly have passed over unseen. At my first stop, by a roadside gravel pit, 27 ringed plovers and one little stint were resting on a sand spit, and as I watched six snipe trotted from behind a headland and joined them. Then, far out over the water, a swarm of black terns was just discernible through the murk, and suddenly they stopped their apparently aimless wavering patrol and headed towards me. One by one they settled on the spit alongside the waders, until 25 lined the edge. Since the remainder were now coasting to and fro at close quarters, a precise count was possible – 45. A visit to the next pit, under the smoking towers of a power station, disclosed my duck counters focusing all their attention (and binoculars) on no less than 71 black terns accompanied by two common or arctic. If this phenomenal visitation was widespread, it will certainly not have escaped nationwide notice.

A COUNTRY DIARY 1975

Oxfordshire: In the flush of fungi induced by the ideal conditions of exceptionally warm soil and plentiful autumn rains, one lowly species, seldom encountered before, became a conspicuous feature, both of rough grassland and in the pastures daily scoured (until the recent frosts) by mushroomers. Many of the latter, intent on the one species of any interest to them, simply failed to see this sudden coating of stems and tufts of grass by a creamy-white granular mass, although one did admit to having thought it odd that blow-flies should lay their eggs on plants, whilst another, viewing a large mass almost completely enveloping a large tussock, came to the inelegant conclusion that 'a dog or fox, or something, had been sick.' The first colony which I noticed had coated a single grass-stem for about six inches up and was about as thick as a pencil. Twenty-four hours later the mass had grown to form a cone some five inches across at the base, and had become greyer. A few days later all that remained was a semi-liquid black mass, dripping its contents to the grass below. This plant (if such it can be called) is slime-fungus (*Mucilago spongiosa*), one of a puzzling group which normally exist as unorganised masses of jelly with no cellular structure, but which, when conditions are right for reproduction, produce organised spore-bearing bodies – and it is the latter which have recently been so obvious. Since the offspring of these 'fruits' can crawl like amoebae and swim like flagellate protozoa, at this stage they behave like primitive forms of animal life rather than as plants.

A COUNTRY DIARY 1976

Oxfordshire: From my house the forest across the valley, less than a mile away, looks drabber than I have ever known it at this season, for there seems to have been a sudden change from green to brown, without the often protracted spell of colour changes in between, and indeed many trees are now already bare. But in this case the belief that 'distance lends enchantment to the view' is refuted, for when seen from within the forest is more colourful than I have ever known it – which is for a period of well over 60 years, the first third of which I spent living in its midst. But the highlights of this autumn spectacular are not created so much by foliage (although the gold of the plentiful native maples is up to standard) as by fruits. The last word is used in its botanical sense, for although the masses of hips and haws contribute the major part of the show, it is the silvery background of old man's beard billowing over trees and bushes which softens the general effect. Viewing this scene from a deep wide bottom in its midst, I became aware that, apart from the superabundance of the berries of hips, haws, sloes and buckthorn berries, a new component in the red parts of the picture, absent in earlier days, was now most conspicuous. This was the abundant spindle, completely clothed in coral cups with the orange seeds exposed. Since, in the old days, spindle rarely matured to fruit, as the young growths were almost invariably barked and killed by rabbits, I believe that its present abundance must have begun with the introduction of myxomatosis.

A COUNTRY DIARY 1977

Oxfordshire: When was the 'goose-summer' which, according to the *OED*, seems to be the only plausible derivation for 'gossamer'? The same entry goes on to say that (perhaps) it was St Martin's summer 'when geese are in season.' But since, in the old-style calendar, this feast would have fallen in what is now the third week of November, much too late for this phenomenon of spider dispersal, I prefer to think that the once traditional Michaelmas goose provides the clue as to season. Appropriately, on a recent Indian summer's day, geese and gossamer literally came into focus together. I was watching a party of about forty Canadas honking across the sky then I became aware of scintillating strands high up in the air, and then noted both sparkling filaments and cottony clots falling on the water. The date was October 13 – almost precisely Old Michaelmas, and on looking at my last year's diary (when a belated redstart in my garden was taking advantage of a similar form of manna) I find that the occurrence was on precisely the same date. Further confirmation is provided by John Ruskin, who, on October 16, 1858, described a fall of gossamer when 'all the fields rippled with a stream of sunshine like a lake, yet no perceptible wind.' But Francis Kilvert's experience of this phenomenon was some five weeks earlier; on September 6, 1875, he records that 'The Virgin's Webs glowed with changing opal lights and glanced with all the colours of the rainbow.'

A COUNTRY DIARY 1978

Oxfordshire: Eight years ago, when I returned here to my old haunts after an absence of almost 30 years, one of the first links with the past was the sighting of a merlin within a stone's throw of my house, at precisely the same spot where I had seen one about 40 years before. But although I was quite certain as to the locality, the picture of the earlier appearance which came to mind somehow did not seem to fit the surroundings as they now were. For the most vivid memory of the first incident was that the merlin kept just ahead of me by a series of short flights, perching on a drystone wall from time to time. The behaviour on this more recent occasion was similar, only this time a tall hedge formed the line of retreat. Beginning to doubt my memory, I looked around to see if any other wall in the neighbourhood might have been the scene of the incident but none was in sight. My memory was vindicated by the discovery of the toppled remnants of a wall within the base of the hedge. All the constituents of the hedge could be attributed to either wind-borne or bird-borne seeds, sycamore, ash and old man's beard in the former category, and hawthorn. elder, crab, spindle, dogrose and wayfaring tree in the latter. Since this initial discovery I have found many other 'self-sown' hedges which have taken over neglected field walls. I now toy with the idea that the first hedges around human enclosures may have had a similar origin before deliberate planting followed, for, from experience with modern equiva- lents, one can be pretty certain that such hedges would spring up at the base of primitive stockades of wooden posts.

A COUNTRY DIARY 1979

Oxfordshire: I thought I had seen the last of our local house martins early on the morning of October 6, when seven, presumably a family party, circled above the roof tops, spiralled up to a great height and set off to disappear in an unexpected direction almost due north-west. But there was one unfortunate non-starter left in one nest when the last late broods took off on the 9th – a youngster, as fully-fledged as it could be, found on the ground beneath a colony near my house. It was in good condition, but incapable of flight because one wing lacked the primary flight-feathers. Fully expecting that it had been mauled by a cat, I was surprised to discover that there was no recent injury but that its wing had been severed at the carpal joint, as a well-healed stump testified. I am at a loss to suggest any possible culprit, for the martin's 'procreant cradle' is pretty well inaccessible to any intruders, apart from other small birds and these, particularly house sparrows and blue tits, enter to take over the premises rather than as direct predators. I have watched a great tit removing newly hatched sparrows from a nest-box one at a time, and a starling picking off young blue-tits in a similar site when they craned their necks up to the entrance-hole in response to the sound of the marauder alighting on the outside. But one would expect that either of these known nest-box predators would have dragged out the whole of the prey, rather than severing a morsel.

A COUNTRY DIARY 1980

Oxfordshire: Year after year the large, apple-shaped hips of *Rosa rugosa* fail to produce the autumn show which I had in mind when I planted the hedge. Fortunately, I planted alternate specimens of sweet briar with them, and these have lived up to their promise to delight both nose and eye. They are now festooned with clusters of small, scarlet hips, as yet unripe, and later will achieve the function for which they were evolved: consumption by birds, mainly blackbirds and thrushes. The *rugosa* certainly produce an abundance of hips, already over-ripe, but as fast as they mature they are torn to pieces instead of being swallowed whole by potential seed-distrib-utors. The explanation is that in this area greenfinches abound, and these, being essentially seed-eaters, attack the hips only to extract and crack the seeds; the ground beneath the tattered remains is littered with husks. Presumably in its native Far East haunts there exists some bird or mammal vector capable of swallowing these large fruits whole, but no such visitor comes to my garden; although seedlings of both sweet briar and *Rosa rubrifolia* – recognisable from scent in the former case, and by the glaucous-mauve foliage in the other – reach the status of common weeds in my garden, I have not so far found a seedling of *rugosa*. My apples provide another example in the same category, but millennia of selective interference by man is responsible for the fact that the original function of the fruit could be consummated only if ostriches existed in our avifauna; the Bramleys I have just picked are larger than my fist and weigh up to three-quarters of a lb each. But, a little farther away there grows an apple – raised from the seed of an ornamental red crab which bears fruit only slightly larger than haws – that is easily consumed by blackbirds at one gulp.

A COUNTRY DIARY 1981

Oxfordshire: Although, for obvious ornithological reasons, I keep no cats, those from neighbouring households appear to prefer the fine tilth always to be found somewhere in my kitchen garden to the toilet facilities available on their home ground. Although they are the undoubted culprits – I have just shooed off one as it began its preliminary excavation on the newly-hoed patch between the lettuce and carrots – it has now been revealed that I have been blaming some of them for another kind of damage for which they are not responsible. Year after year one large tuffet of thrift begins to turn brown in the centre, and the dead patch spreads outwards, so that in late summer only a fringe of living green survives on a clump as large as a cushion. Yet another plant, only a few yards away, is a thriving mass of greenery. One could only assume that the affected plant was being regularly visited by some animal and naturally – having only too often seen the other natural function fulfilled – I jumped to the conclusion that a cat was poisoning or scalding the foliage. Now, directly because of the 'anting' of the starlings recorded here a few weeks ago, puss has been exonerated. Having observed that the patch of the lawn from which the ants were emerging was completely bleached and dead, I straightaway thought of the thrift, and a poke with a stick into the heart of the cushion brought out black ants by the myriad. I cannot account for this difference between black ants and their by-products and those of the mound-building yellow species, for on downland the hillocks of the latter are clothed in wild thyme or rockrose.

A COUNTRY DIARY 1982

Oxfordshire: I returned home, after having enjoyed, during my Portland visit, the sight of my first clouded yellow butterflies for many years, and the convolvulus hawk-moth which was my second ever (the first proudly brought in from the greenhouse, uninjured, by a very soft-mouthed cocker spaniel, over fifty years ago, in my present locality), to find that another splendid immigrant from the continent, the death's-head hawk-moth, must have penetrated as far inland as Oxfordshire many weeks ago. Two huge caterpillars found feeding on potato leaves in a garden a few miles from Oxford City were eventually collected by a friend. They were full-grown – about as large as an average man's forefinger – bright yellowish-green in colour, with seven purplish-blue stripes on either side uniting on the back to form a series of Vs, and, as with most caterpillars of this family, having a curved 'horn' on the tail. It is practically certain that such specimens are the offspring of immigrant parents, for the pupae, buried in the soil, are not known to overwinter successfully in our climate. But (again harking back to the good old days of fifty-odd years ago) the death's-head was once far from uncommon and I frequently saw specimens found during potato-lifting. If, as sometimes happened, the perfect moth (with its 5-inch wingspan, skull and crossbones pattern on its thorax, and its ability to squeak like a mouse, combining to make it an object of super-stitious dread) entered a house, it was likely to be summarily dispatched – the first which I saw had been killed in a lighted bedroom by a clout from the bedside Bible. Since potato-haulm is now usually sprayed to burn it off before harvesting, potato-fields are no longer good habitats for the larvae, and unsprayed garden patches are the likeliest sites.

A COUNTRY DIARY 1983

Oxfordshire: Although I have often watched our smallest seabirds – storm petrels – appearing like bats at dusk around their nesting burrows on Pembrokeshire islands and the Shetlands, I have yet to see one of their larger and rarer relatives, Leach's or the fork-tailed petrel, on the wing. Therefore, I was somewhat peeved to discover, on my recent visit to Portland, that if I had gone straight down to do a sea-watch at the Bill on arrival – instead of concentrating on the melodious warbler in the observatory garden – I could have seen my first live specimen close inshore. But I was even more exasperated to learn, on my arrival back inland, that at least two specimens had been driven this far inland, one seen briefly at a reservoir, and the other watched for a longer period at a gravel-pit, both of which sites I visit regularly. Since there was a large concentration of these storm-driven birds off the Cornish coast during these early September gales – forced back from the oceanic feeding-grounds to which they would be migrating – it seems likely that a 'wreck' of these featherweight mites (a well-fed specimen would barely scale a couple of ounces) may have occurred. The last such catastrophe was in October 1952, when I was brought a corpse found in the mouth of a rabbit burrow near my Berkshire home. This turned out to be just one of 6,700 such known casualties recorded not only throughout Great Britain and Ireland, but also as far afield as Switzerland and Germany.

A COUNTRY DIARY 1984

Oxfordshire: Serendipity (which, according to the *OED*, is 'the faculty of making happy and unexpected discoveries by accident') has caused me to change my theme for this week. I had set out for a ramble in my local woodland haunts, with the autumn tints and berries of a favourite section of the forest in mind, and proceeded for about half a mile, noting the colour changes on elder, hawthorn and spindle, and being particularly impressed by the fact that the ashes, which drop their leaves at the first real air-frost, were still the greenest trees outstanding in the mellowing mantle of oaks, maple, sycamore and beech. Then I noticed a large tree high up on the bank which had never caught my eye before, although I must have passed the site hundreds of times in the last 74 years. There had been some clearing of the edge of the ride in preparation for the pheasant-shooting season, and presumably this had opened up the view. My first impression, from its form, was that the tree was an apple, but its huge size seemed not to fit. But a glance through binoculars revealed that my guess was correct, for small apples still hung on some of the twigs. Pushing my way through head-high bracken, and sampling the fallen fruits I was left in no doubt as to the status of this tree – a genuine wild crab, unlike many wildings which bear evidence of garden ancestry. A rough estimate of its height suggested that its crown was at least 60 feet above ground-level, in which case it may turn out to be a record specimen. But its girth at eye-level, measured by encircling the trunk by a thin, whippy hazel wand from a nearby bush, was a mere 5ft 6ins, well below the record in this respect.

A COUNTRY DIARY 1985

Oxfordshire: Continuing my scanning of the sky in search of departing martins or swallows, on the idyllic Indian summery day of October 13, it became evident that starlings had deserted the elders, on whose berries they had been gorging for the past few weeks, in pursuit of some aerial prey. When so engaged, and particularly, as on this occasion at a considerable height, such is their acrobatic expertise that these otherwise clumsy and ungainly movers could be mistaken for swallows or martins. But the puzzling feature of this activity was that there was no visible evidence of an abundance of insects on the wing, as there was when some weeks ago the air swarmed with daddy-long-legs and flying ants. Then, as the day went on, it became evident that a fall of gossamer was occurring, and by late afternoon, lit by a low sun, the nearby playing field was completely carpeted by an iridescent film of the silky material, suggesting a calm and somewhat oily sea viewed against a setting sun. There must have been a truly phenomenal fall, and, as one's shoes became encased in the web, one's thoughts turned to a similar fall 244 years ago, when Gilbert White's early morning 'field diversion' was frustrated because his dogs were 'so blinded and hoodwinked that they could not proceed, but were obliged to lie down and scrape the encumbrances from their faces with their forefeet.' Since I have observed starlings feeding on plum aphids, it seems quite feasible that they might have been feeding on the minute spiders, which are not only considerably larger items than aphids, but also must have been available by the million.

A COUNTRY DIARY 1986

Oxfordshire: Earlier this year, when it became apparent from the failure of hawthorn to bloom that the fieldfares, redwings and blackbirds arriving from the continent would be deprived of perhaps the most important item of their winter diet, I assumed that they would perforce have to turn their attention to the abundant crop of hips on both dog and field roses. I certainly did not expect to see my first local party, in the first week of this month, feeding on still abundant and unwithered elderberries. Despite mass attacks by starlings as soon as they were ripe, possibly because these birds later turned their attention to invertebrates such as leather-jackets in grassland, many elders are still laden with sound berries, and this exceptionally extended season of availability seems general, as I noticed all along the route to East Anglia and back on my recent visit. On the other hand, some berry-bearing species which, in my experience, are usually some of the last to be exploited by birds, have already been stripped. Last year blackbirds were still feeding in my garden on the white berries of two Asiatic species of Sorbus (*S. hupehensis* and *S. cashmiriana*) well after Christmas, but, despite the abundance of windfall apples available, the 'blackies' have just about cleared them already.

A COUNTRY DIARY 1987

Portland Bill: Emigratory passage here has been spasmodic. One day the place was swarming with migrants: willow warblers in their hundreds accompanied by a few other species such as redstarts, garden warblers, and spotted flycatchers. But the most phenomenal 'fall' became apparent on the morning of August 25 when, after a night of strong north-westerly wind, the island was alive with wheatears. Counts in various fields suggested that several hundred, if not more than a thousand, were involved. Among these were some outstandingly handsome males, both in size and colour, which suggested that at least some of the influx were birds of the northern race, probably from as far afield as Greenland. On comparatively birdless days I amused myself by trying to assess the numbers of some of the more colourful butterflies concentrated on a continuous edging of golden samphire in full bloom on the East Cliff. On a stretch of about two hundred yards my best score so far has been more than 500 small tortoiseshells, 14 painted ladies, 20 red admirals and 7 clouded yellows. But strangely not a single specimen of peacock, which was by far the commonest of this group at home on my buddleias. Although birds have been going out, other migrants have been coming in: on the day of my arrival a fine specimen of the convolvulus hawk-moth had been trapped.

A COUNTRY DIARY 1988

Oxfordshire: On my pre-breakfast scanning of the sky above my garden on October 2, I witnessed what will probably be the final passage of departing house martins. High up to the north and extending as far as I could see from horizon to horizon, the sky was speckled with widely spaced birds, and although at first they appeared to be randomly circling and making little progress, within a few minutes they were overhead and five minutes later they had all disappeared towards the south-west. But whilst I was watching there came a reminder that this was the season of arrival as well as of departure, for a party of seven redwings, my first for this autumn, flew overhead. Then, for good measure, the small birds active in the Lawson cypress just across the lane from my garden turned out to be a party of seven siskins, busily probing the heavy crop of small cones on one tree. These are regular winter visitors to the alders along the Evenlode down in the valley about a mile away, but it is a new experience to be able to watch them daily from the kitchen-sink window – my latest count, four days after their arrival, is of ten. The widespread planting of the conifer in question (much criticised not only on aesthetic grounds, but also because the planters fail to realise the long-term climax of forest trees with a potential height of around 120 feet), now that many of them are mature enough to bear cones, is likely to prove beneficial as an alternative source of food to the winter-visiting siskins which normally rely on birch and alder. Another winter visitor with similar tastes, the redpoll, has, during the last few years, also frequented the same clump of cypresses, usually after having stripped the seed-catkins of my birch.

A COUNTRY DIARY 1989

Oxfordshire: On the night of the last full moon I awoke somewhere around 3am, and for a moment thought that I must still be dreaming, for I could hear the guttural groaning of fallow deer, punctuated by final higher-pitched barking calls, as if they were just outside my bedroom, as they were literally when I first heard them from the same site almost 80 years ago. The rutting season is now well under way, and although I am now about a mile away from the deer-park, westerly winds bring the news of what is in progress clearly across the Evenlode Valley. Since I hear the continuous clamour both by day and night, it would seem that, apart from having little time for feeding, the amorous bucks also do without sleep, both factors contributing to their poor condition after the rut. Unfortunately, however, I have been somewhat circumscribed in getting much further afield than the garden, owing to a foot injury, and therefore have had time to read by daylight – an unusual experience for me. Three more books have been added to the excellent Natural History series of Whittet Books (£6.95). These include *Snakes and Lizards*, by Tom

Langton; and *Eagles*, by John A. Love, dealing particularly with our native golden eagle and the reintroduced former native, the sea-eagle, the author having been for many years involved with the now successful re-estab- lishment of the latter. *Stoats & Weasels, Polecats & Pine-Martens*, by Paddy Seelman, is again a work based on first-hand research, some of it on Irish stoats, confusingly known as weasels in the island where this smallest member of the family does not occur. [Of these books, only *Eagles* is still in print, price £9.99. Ed.]

A COUNTRY DIARY 1990

Oxfordshire: Now that the wind is westerly, from time to time I hear evocative sounds from the deer-park about a mile away – the long-drawn- out grunting and groaning of the rutting bucks, and the clash of antlers in the ensuing combats. For 21 of my early years I lived with this herd ('emparked' by a wall about 600 years ago) just outside our cottage, and remember the thrill of finding a new-born fawn in the bracken nearby. But since then my attitude to fallow deer has changed, for during the last war years, when the park became a military transport depot, some of the herd escaped and colonised the adjacent forest of Wychwood, with disas- trous results for some of the rarer flora – orchids in particular seem to be relished in the flower-bud stage, and even the poisonous stinking helle- bore gets denuded of its blossoms. It is therefore high praise when I can still, despite this botanical bias, enjoy a book mainly concerned with the pleasures of deer-watching – not only fallows, but also our magnificent red native, and the charming and cheeky little roe, but also newcomers such as sika and muntjac. This is *A Watcher in the Woods*, by Patricia Sibley, Whittet Books, £9.95. [Out of print. Ed.] But, apart from the main theme, a wide range of flora and fauna encountered in deer- watching comes within the scope of this meticulous and patient observer, recorded in beautiful prose, often in short, staccato sentences which somehow convey excitement. Even my bête noire, the grey squirrel, which displaced our once plentiful native red squirrel (one of which used to come in to feed on the remnants on our cat's plate, through the ever- open back-door) is revealed as an interesting woodland occupant, but I cannot forgive it for its uneconomic habit, noted by the author, of 'strip- ping a hazel of its frilly green nut-cases, when it was too early for a single one to have grown a kernel.'

A COUNTRY DIARY 1991

Oxfordshire: Earlier this month, feeling more confident after two excursions to gather sloes for making a few bottles of the comforting liqueur, I offered to take a visitor from Australia, who was keen to see Wychwood from the inside, into The Forest, and managed to penetrate about half a mile down a wide ride with only the occasional pause for breath. Autumn colours had suddenly appeared, but in bright sunlight the most striking effect was that the oaks, the predominant large trees, had their wide range of brownish tints embellished, almost to their crowns, by the silvery pappus of old man's beard. Another interesting feature, suggesting mini-climates dependant on both light and soil conditions arising from exposure or shading in sunlight, was that on one side of the broad ride the fringe of bracken was still a pale yellowish green, whilst on the other the verge was of rusty brown and shrivelled fronds. As we proceeded, scores of pheasants gradually withdrew into cover, but when we reached the area where most had assembled, a faint chirping came from beneath a nearby bush, and a young cock, with tail not yet full-grown, emerged, and still uttering plaintive food-calls, came right up to our feet, and we were soon surrounded by others following its bold example. Obviously they associated humans with friendly visits from keepers distributing grain, but within a few weeks will have cause to know that other human visitors have less friendly intentions. By a coincidence I discovered that this problem of coddling game-birds and then expecting them to be wild enough to shoot by November was nothing new, for on the night of the same day I happened to switch on to the BBC World Service and there seemed to be a programme based on literary references to this season – and the one for November 8, 1879 was a diary entry from Thomas Hardy (who admired me in my pram) recording that when that day he had entered a keeper's cottage, an attendant party of young pheasants had followed him in.

A COUNTRY DIARY 1992

Oxfordshire: The first week in this month enlivened my somewhat static and humdrum existence. Firstly came a visit from the BBC's Panorama team. Although part of a programme planned to discuss a local controversial building development, I was brought in because the site is separated from my garden only by a narrow lane and especially because the field concerned had for 20-odd years provided my pre-breakfast walks and my most prolific bird-catching site for ringing purposes. (The programme should be screened on BBC1 on September 21.) Next came a visit to the school from which I retired as headmaster 22 years ago, after a spell of 21 years, for the opening ceremony to celebrate the conversion of the redundant building as a day centre with residential homes for elderly parishioners. The last treat was when a fellow voluntary warden of the Wychwood Nature Reserve took me to The Forest to see if what he called 'the naked ladies' were in bloom. They were in abundance. I still know this plant as autumn crocus, in spite of many boyhood corrections from pedantic botanists, one of whom, a local village schoolmaster, preferred the name meadow saffron. This was just as inaccurate, for saffron is a crocus and this plant, a *Colchicum*, belonging to the lily family, is not a member of the iris family to which the true crocuses belong. But of all the excitements of the week, the high was the sight of a colony of the parasitic greater dodder on a slight deviation from the main road to a minor road near Dorchester-on-Thames on the way home. Appropriately the plants were on the two plants mentioned in text-book as favourite hosts – nettles at the hedge bottom, transferring to the climbing hop-bines higher up. This is a rare plant locally but here it was abundant, sprawling over many yards of the hedge. After the initial seedling has found a host, the root is no longer necessary, for the bunches of tiny pink flowers draw their sustenance from their host, to which they are attached by thread-like pink stems.

A COUNTRY DIARY 1993

Oxfordshire: A chance to visit Farmoor about ten days ago was eagerly accepted. On arrival the water was dead calm, and apart from a party of a few hundred tufted duck and a scattering of mallard, great crested grebe, 30 odd cormorants, and five little grebe, there appeared to be nothing of interest, for even the expected swallows and martins failed to show. Then my companion spotted some waders in the far distance on the windward side of an embankment, where the lapping water was probably bringing in food. At first the party seemed to consist of two dunlin and five little stints, but a prolonged search at closer quarters increased the score to five and ten respectively; then the birds rose and passed in a flock, and I estimated the total as 20. The party then settled, and my rapid count proved nearly correct, for there were nine dunlin accompanied by 12 little stints. These two species are often associated on passage migration, and since the stint is not a native breeding species, it seems likely that both of these waders are from somewhere to the north. A bit further on we flushed six common sandpipers, and finally finished with a close-up of three ruffs, or to be pedantically correct, one ruff and two reeves. But eventually the distinction of the sexes will disappear, for in my early days mallard was confined to the drake of the female and the latter was merely a wild duck. Now, mallard covers the species as a whole. Whilst engaged in wader-spotting, we became aware of the increasing number of wagtails on the move, mainly pied, but with a good sprinkling of yellows. The first swallow appeared, followed by a few others, and scores of sand martins with a few house martins. The sight of dunlin and little stints together reminded me of an incident at precisely the same site some years ago. On this occasion a single dunlin was followed wherever it went by a much tinier little stint – and a nearby angler (no ornithologist) remarked that it was nice to see that these birds brought their young ones with them on their annual visits.

A COUNTRY DIARY 1994

Charlbury, Oxfordshire: There is no doubt that the most interesting thing that has happened within the last few weeks is that a single starling has frequently appeared on a peanut bag and stayed for some time, which has excluded tits and greenfinches. This may sound trivial but is puzzling, for I have never come across this phenomenon before. This is puzzling because the starling has claws like talons; as I learnt only too well when I used to catch them for ringing in mist nets, when each claw used to have to be extracted singularly, so it cannot be that a lack of clinging ability was responsible. Presumably the same bird has returned several times each day. On mentioning this to others who have peanut bags, I find that it is not at all unusual behaviour, for some feeders repeatedly get starlings on their peanut bags. The other interesting happening took place last week and arose from a replaying of tapes for radio programmes made some 20 years ago. The precise year of the one being listened to was 1976 and mainly concentrated on the drought, which almost reduced the lake at Blenheim to a sheet of mud with very occasional shallow pools of water.

As I listened I found myself thinking not 'liar' but 'fibber'! For the narrator was using my exact words as though he had experienced the events personally. For example, he reported how he had caught and ringed house martins over my neighbour's swimming pool, and how the following year one of them nested at Tring on the house of the organiser of the British Bird Ringing Scheme.

When the tape had finished I expressed my opinion of the verity of the speaker and received the reply, 'But that was you speaking'!

13

COUNTRY DIARIES – WINTER

A COUNTRY DIARY 1964

Hertfordshire: This year, to forestall sceptical remarks which have been known to include references to viewing the world through rose-coloured (or more bluntly, wine-tinted) binoculars, I decided to do my bird-watching after breakfast on Christmas Day rather than after lunch. As I set out, I paused to look at the split in the old damson tree where the wryneck used to nest, and immediately a starling was about my ears uttering clinking notes of solicitude and disapproval. A few feathers and straws protruding from the crevice, and sounds of subdued starling chatter from within, caused me to turn back to get a ladder. Before I could look in, three perfectly mature starlings flew out. From their white-speckled plumage, and the anxiety of the glossier adult who now joined them, it seems that this was a family party still using its nesting-site as a snug roost. This non-conformism of a small minority of starlings, when the vast majority of wintering birds of their kind are leading a life of communal feeding and roosting, can be seen at its most strong-minded when excited hordes of starlings gathering on the way to roost happen to settle in the immediate vicinity of the stay-at-home birds. One would think that these would be pulled in by the mass-magnetism which seems to control such aggregations, but they remain completely indifferent; indeed, if there is any reaction, it seems to be one of self-assertion in the face of tremendous odds, for one veteran resident at my Berkshire home, on such occasions, takes a firm stance on the roof-ridge and goes through his repertoire of imitations – lapwing, broody hen, partridge, circular saw and telephone bell.

A COUNTRY DIARY 1965

Berkshire: The heavy crop of haws had already been considerably thinned by our native thrushes, mainly blackbirds, many weeks before the arrival of their northern relatives, the fieldfares and redwings. Now the hedges are completely stripped, and the change in the weather has occurred just in time for members of this adaptable family to switch to the ground as a source of food. At last the low-lying meadows (where the moles turn up former marsh-soil as black as jet) are waterlogged, and one ridge-and-furrow pasture is now marked out with long parallel pools, precisely one chain apart.

A week ago, before the peaty layer above the clay had become saturated, this field and its surrounding hedges were practically birdless. Today, in spite of the wind and the rain, it contained a higher population of birds than I have ever seen before. The musical, contented creaking of teal (the first of the season here), the chuckles and squeaks of redwings and fieldfare, and the querulous bickering chatter of starlings, could be heard long before I reached the gap in the dense hedge.

There were about eighty teal swimming in the gullies or paddling in the soggy herbage, a few scattered pairs of mallard, and a continuous shuttle-service of fieldfares and redwings between the ground and the hedges. Overhead a straggling but well-disciplined flock of lapwings, estimated at some two thousand, carried out seemingly aimless manoeuvres, and quite as many wood pigeons (also the first mass assembly of the season) streamed to the westward into the wind. As I neared home, in worsening weather, a passer-by commiserated, 'Not much of a day for bird-watching.'

A COUNTRY DIARY 1966/67

Berkshire: Now that foot-and-mouth disease is only one county away from here, my neighbour, looking out on thousands of starlings and hundreds of gulls and lapwing among his Herefords, must view the scene with some trepidation – particularly if he has just been informed by the farming reporter of his Sunday newspaper that 'it is generally accepted but so far unproved, that the disease is carried by birds, principally starlings, and in coastal areas by sea-gulls.' On the face of it the assumption seems logical; twice a year our island is invaded by species which have a marked preference for the company of cattle, and these have either come from or passed through areas of Europe where foot-and-mouth is endemic. On these grounds one would expect outbreaks to occur in the south with the arrival of yellow wagtails in April, and, on a much greater scale, with the arrival of starlings from Baltic regions in autumn. But nothing resembling this pattern is revealed from a study of the very detailed statistics of epidemics in Britain. About fifteen years ago (in a review of a work by veterinarians who were plainly not ornithologists) Richard Fitter made it clear, from an analysis of the known facts, that the verdict was 'not likely' rather than 'not proven'. The most significant point in this review, highly suggestive that man (or his cargo) was the virus-carrier, was the fact that the scourge practically ceased with the curtailment of shipping during the war-years – but starlings still plied to and fro across the North Sea.

A COUNTRY DIARY 1967

Berkshire: : I used to regard stories of bats consuming the fat from bacon hanging in the old open chimneys as folk-lore, on a par with the mythical propensity of these web-fingered mammals to entangle themselves in ladies' hair. But my scepticism as to a bat's ability to gnaw or nibble at large masses of food vanished recently when the church organ was removed for repairs: in a recess behind I found the remains of a candle, still upright, but a mere tapering cone surrounding the intact wick. The nature of the erosion did not suggest the work of mice or other rodents, but the possible identity of the consumer did not occur to me until I made a closer examination of the debris around the candle-stump – the accumulated droppings of a bat (or bats). A year ago more serious erosion was discovered in the main timbers of the tower and bell-turret, for all that was left of once stout baulks of oak was the central 'wick' of heartwood, no thicker than my wrist; the larvae of both deathwatch and furniture beetles had consumed the main bulk of the beams – the sapwoood. Repairs have just been completed, and, judging by the jubilant change-ringing on the peal of eight bells yesterday, the ringers have been indulging in secret practice during the silent period.

A COUNTRY DIARY 1968/69

Berkshire: Today, January 5, a cock blackcap was feeding on apples in my garden even before it was light enough for the regular visitors – blackbirds and fieldfares – to attend for the same purpose. Not many years ago some incredulous ornithologists were inclined to dismiss such midwinter records of this summer migrant as cases of mistaken identity, considering that the black-headed birds were nothing more unusual than marsh tits.

The weakness of this argument was that it did not account for winter records of female blackcaps, which have distinctive brown caps. Since those doubting days the presence of blackcaps in winter has been accepted as a fact, confirmed (as in this present instance) by examination of the bird in the hand. But there is one particular aspect of these winter occurrences which suggests that they represent something more than stray birds which failed to emigrate with the bulk of their species in August and September, namely that the vast majority of such records are for December, January and February. If these were merely left-overs from the previous breeding season one would expect continuous records. The only explanation seems to be that from some unknown source there is a winter influx into Britain – possibly, and surprisingly, on the evidence of one ringed bird, from Central Europe.

A COUNTRY DIARY 1969

Berkshire: A few weeks ago I wrote of the drying-up of our fishpond, due to the subsidence of its bed following pumping operations taking water and silt from the substratum in a neighbouring field. Now that the cause of the depletion has ceased the pond is slowly reverting to its former state, but it seems that it is filling upwards through the dry-crusted ooze, and the chief evidence for this is that a transit on foot is now a stickier business, and one's deep footprints rapidly fill with water. But at one point, right in the centre of the main expanse of exposed muddy bed, a shallow pool had appeared, even before the rains came to augment it. This has been a regular haunt for that welcome and elegant winter-visitor, the grey wagtail, and in watching one through binoculars recently I was surprised to find that the mere puddle was already seething with sticklebacks. A few weeks ago these had been confined to a final concentration in the only undrained gully, and had supplied easy meat to heron and kingfisher whilst still active, and for carrion crows when dead or moribund from lack of oxygen. I am certain, having watched this pond daily for several months, that no water has reached this newly-formed puddle from any possible stickleback haunts, and the only conclusion seems to be that sticklebacks, like tench, can suspend animation and await the return of more normal conditions in mud. I can find no confirmation of this from any text book, and would welcome any comments from knowledgeable readers.

A COUNTRY DIARY 1970

Oxfordshire: After an absence of twenty-eight years, I have returned to settle on the fringe of the Cotswolds in West Oxfordshire – overlooking the ancient forest of Wychwood, in the midst of which I spent my childhood and early manhood, and, most important of all, where, quite unconsciously, my interest in natural history began. I feel quite at home even after one week, and I have come to the conclusion that the basic reason for this is geological. When one has spent the impressionable years of one's life (in this case from five to thirty-seven) in an environment dominated by limestone houses, field-walls, stiles, gate-posts and uneven floors – red brick seems unnatural and therefore unhomely. But, hastening to excavate holes for fruit-trees and shrubs, I have rediscovered the fact that the beloved oolite is not so tractable as chalk, particularly for the more than middle-aged gardener. At one spit deep the flaky weathered upper stratum of the limestone is encountered, and sometimes the fork (hereabouts still a 'digger') has to be laid aside to make way for the pick-axe (a 'peck'). Whoever coined the phrase 'as different as chalk from cheese' was no gardener; in the garden which I have just vacated the marly-chalk was very like cheese, and one could cut through it for several feet deep with no other tool than a sharp spade.

A COUNTRY DIARY 1971

Berkshire: Some two hundred years ago, the Reverend Gilbert White, choosing his words with typical delicacy, made the observation that earthworms 'are much addicted to venery'. On many mornings recently, in spite of almost freezing temperatures, many pairs of earthworms, with their tail-ends in adjacent burrows, have been observed with their foreparts 'locked in the ultimate embrace' on the surface not only of the lawn, but also on the bare earth. The operation is not, in fact, the passionate affair which White's coy description suggests – since worms are hermaphrodite, all that is taking place is the mutual exchange of sperms, which will later be used to fertilise the eggs laid in the leathery greenish-brown capsules. But the interest of this procedure is that for its sluggish duration – which may be for a whole day – the participants seem to become immune to the normally alarming advent of daylight; even more extraordinary seems to be the immunity from the attention of the early bird, traditionally apt to snatch the partially surfaced worm just before sunrise has had its warming effect on the light-sensitive skin. I have repeatedly noted one of my backdoor blackbirds, on its usual early-morning patrol of the path outside, pass within a foot or so of immobile and fully exposed earthworms, and leave them to it with (apparently) a chivalrous averting of the eye.

A COUNTRY DIARY 1972

Oxfordshire: At about this time last year I passed a field boundary along the edge of which I used to cycle to work about 40 years ago, and was amazed at the transformation which had occurred during my absence, and indeed was puzzled in trying to recall its former state. Eventually I had to investigate to confirm my recollection of the latter, for what had once been a bare extent of dry-stone wall was now a continuous billowy mass of old man's beard, with its fleecy fruits glinting like gossamer in the sunlight. In this sunshine today the visual effect was even more striking, for a strong wind was accentuating the momentary gleams from the silky hairs. But in the meantime I have discovered that one traveller's joy may be another man's eyesore, for last spring I met an old man who, recognising me, began to bewail the changes for the worse which had occurred during my long absence. 'Have you seen what has happened to the wall along Hazel Wood Field? Yent that a disgrace? Can't see a single stwun along what used to be about ten chain of good walling.'

Meanwhile the old man's beard continues to exploit bare territories, and at a pace which has surprised me; our local railway line was reduced to a single track about a year ago, and on one section, near a woodland fringe, this wild clematis has already made a carpet of about 10 feet wide to cover the bare ballast left when the rails were lifted.

A COUNTRY DIARY 1973

Oxfordshire: In an area where evidence of the traditional use of the underlying limestone still abounds – in the form of roofing slates, floor slabs, kitchen sinks, non-creaking stairs, field gate-posts, drinking troughs, and of course the obvious stone-built houses and field walls – it may seem strange that the disappearance of a single lump of limestone has caused a good deal of local controversy. As the chairman said at a recent parish council meeting: 'All you people who are making so much fuss about this stone should have spoken up in the first place, before it was lost.'

Although this statement may in itself appear to be another gem (or precious stone) of hindsight-inspired wisdom, it contains more than a grain of truth. The sad fact is that the vast majority of residents in our ancient little township were unaware of the existence of this old stone, some 5ft high and weighing at least a couple of tons, which stood just across the brook at the edge of the sewage disposal works. It was one of several, and a local antiquarian pronounced it to be a Saxon 'mark-stone', one of several such delineating the boundaries of the original pre-conquest settlement. From his researches it appears that such markers were set up around the town at intervals of about three quarters of a mile.

A COUNTRY DIARY 1974

Oxfordshire: In spite of its precocious blooming the commonly grown ornamental almond, even when absence of bullfinch predation results in a mass of pink bloom, rarely produces heavy crops of fruit; usually either lack of insect pollinators at the critical time, or late frosts when the fruits are just forming, are to blame. But this season has been exceptional for fruit production on almonds, and the hundreds hanging on otherwise bare twigs now add an unfamiliar aspect to the silhouettes of trees in many gardens and parks. My neighbour has two such specimens conveniently overhanging his wall, and some weeks ago the first splitting fruits invited interior inspection of the wrinkled nuts exposed. At first I had in mind a cheap substitute for shelled peanuts in the shape of almond kernels for use on my bird table, when I resorted to a hammer after having bent the nut crackers, but I changed my mind after peeling and tasting the first plump kernel, for these were veritable sweet almonds. The presence of this neglected crop going to waste under his nose was pointed out to the rightful owner, and my own formerly minor depredations were legitimised and proceeded on a grander scale. But one word of warning to prospective almond harvesters – although many of the common ornamental kinds are of the true sweet species, other bitter-nutted kinds are also common, among the latter a large-flowered peace-almond hybrid. Since the nutcracker himself has a bruised thumb to bear witness to his activities, it is inevitable that, this year, both Christmas pudding and mincemeat containing fresher chopped almonds than ever before will be referred to as 'the nutcracker's sweet.'

A COUNTRY DIARY 1975

Oxfordshire: Some of our local gravel-pit pools are so extensive that picking out strangers amongst the packed congregations of the commoner duck species – mallard. tufted, pochard, teal, and wigeon – is often as difficult as sea-watching, for in some weather conditions ripples and wave motion produce the same sort of frustrating momentary appearances and disappearances of birds on the surface. On a recent scanning of such a winter gathering the six goosanders were not difficult to find, simply because the two splendid drakes were much more conspicuous than the commoner ducks around them. A few days previously, in foggy conditions, a 'duck' on floodwater in the Windrush Valley provided me with a more difficult problem of identification. It was in a party of six, all periodically up-ending in a very splashing manner, and it was the only one which I was able to get a reasonable view of before they disappeared into the mist. All I could record was that it was a dumpy brownish duck with pale cheeks and under parts. Racking my brains, all I could think of were quite improbable species such as females of either common scoter or long-tailed duck. On the return journey the flotilla was a little nearer, but I was still unable to get a satisfactory view. Then, conveniently, a moorhen swam close by the mysterious birds and immediately they revealed their true identity – dabchicks or little grebes. This shaming revelation stresses the importance of relative size – before the moorhen appeared on the featureless expanse of water and mist no standard for comparison had been available and, of course, I had been misled by the inelegant diving behaviour. The few inches of water were apparently insufficient for the usual neat 'plop' disappearing act of the dabchick.

A COUNTRY DIARY 1976

Oxfordshire: A few weeks ago I chanced to encounter two friends, or at least one friend and acquaintance, on a BBC Nationwide programme. The first, Clifford Christie, the author of *And Then They Fly Away* (the story of his highly successful work as an amateur 'bird doctor') was immediately recognisable, but the second, a magnificent long-eared owl staring haughtily into the camera with luminous orange-amber eyes, bore little resemblance to the bedraggled, broken-winged creature found floundering in a hedge bottom near my house about a year ago. At that time reports from all over Britain indicated that there had been a huge influx of these birds, but apart from knowing that they had come from across the North Sea (confirmed by reports from coastal observatories) one could do no more than hazard a guess as to the probable starting point of their emigratory journey.

The current number of the British Trust for Ornithology's monthly news-sheet announces two recoveries of ringed long-eared owls last spring, in Dorset and Cambridge. Each had been ringed in Latvia. 'Tufty', as my casualty has been named, can now fly, and has undergone the patient and protracted treatment – amounting to occupational therapy – which is so essential for rehabilitation. He will not be released into the wild until the spring, either to set a course for his presumed Baltic home-land or to find a mate among our very sparse local population.

A COUNTRY DIARY 1977

Oxfordshire: Even immediately after leaf-fall, the old alders along the brook looked pretty dense against the sky, for every twig was studded with blackish cones. Now their silhouettes are daily growing more solid, for the masses of purple catkins are already half-grown. But the odd feature this season is that so far the bumper crop of seed is not being exploited by the expected winter visitors, namely the two small finches – siskins and redpolls – which are sufficiently light and agile to cling to the cone-like fruits. In the case of the siskins, reports from several sources seem to suggest that they have not invaded in their usual number, but, not a mile away from the alders, redpolls are present in force. Normally I see the odd specimen in my neighbourhood amongst the mixed finch flocks on weedy stubble, and last year for a few days a record party of five or six was present. But now from time to time the twanging metallic twittering of redpolls in flight, or sunning themselves on the topmost twigs of the dead elms, can be heard from my doorstep.

A COUNTRY DIARY 1978

Oxfordshire: Recently a friend, driving along a very busy main road near Oxford, noticed the apparent corpse of a bird traffic-casualty in his path, and rather from curiosity as to its identity than from any other motive, pulled off the road at the next convenient point and walked back to retrieve it. Before the opportunity for a safe venture into the road occurred, no less than three juggernaut lorries and eight cars had passed over the object of his curiosity, which turned out to be a still warm, but ostensibly lifeless, female sparrow-hawk.

The body was placed in a cardboard box, and on this being opened at the end of the journey, a very much alive and alert sparrow-hawk was standing to meet the eyes of the surprised rescuer. The only obvious injury was the avian equivalent of a black-eye, but since binocular vision is essential for this dashing predator, the bird was not released.

Instead it was taken to another friend – Cliff Christie, renowned locally for his skill and patience in doctoring, nursing and (a factor often overlooked by well-meaning exponents of such good works) rehabilitating injured birds. Now, just 10 days after the accident, the bird, in fine fettle after a diet of four mice per day, and with vision unimpaired, has been released near the point where it was found – again an often overlooked culmination to successful treatment, but important when the patient has been brought in from any distance.

Direct impact with a vehicle may have concussed this bird, but experience gained by this 'bird-doctor' in dealing with all-too-many such traffic-victims, as well as personal observation of one incident, leads him to suspect that often the bird is thrown out of control in the turbulent air-currents created by speeding vehicles.

A COUNTRY DIARY 1979

Oxfordshire: It must have been over a decade ago that I wrote a Diary from Berkshire illustrating the point that the concept of litter is a very subjective reaction to matter which appears to be objectionably out of place. On that occasion I had risen early one summer dawn to find the school playing-field (through which a right-of-way existed) littered with large greyish-white fragments which, I concluded, could only be the newspaper wrappings from what must have been a veritable mass orgy of fish and chips on the previous night. Closer inspection, with the low rays of the rising sun lighting up the scene from another angle, revealed the beautiful reality – the turf was 'sullied' by nothing worse than sheets of dew-spangled cobwebs. I have just had a similar experience whilst walking along the brookside path in search of siskins. The hauling out of dead elms has transformed a narrow footpath into a wide track of hard, compacted earth, and on this, for 20 yards or so, there was a trail of what appeared to be fragments of orange-peel. Once again offensive 'litter' became acceptable when it was realised that it was a perfectly natural and legitimate adornment of the bare track – the orange-peel fungus, *otidia aurantia* – now, I gather renamed *Aleuria*; but the older name, referring to ear-like shape and orange colour is the one which, on account of its aptness, sticks in my memory.

A COUNTRY DIARY 1980/81

Oxfordshire: News of a large party of whooper swans at the now traditional site in the Upper Cherwell Valley came just as increased flooding made a towpath walk somewhat risky and so – luckily as it turned out – I waited a couple of days before making my annual midwinter visit. I could not have timed my early-morning visit better for, after a drive through dull and showery conditions, my descent into the valley brought me beneath an almost clear sky, and already the distant floodwater belied its actual muddy state by appearing as clean and bright as mirrors. After drawing a blank at one favoured site, I walked upstream along the canal and eventually came across what I sought in a secluded corner of floodwater: 11 pure white adult whoopers with three dingier juveniles. For good measure, immediately in front of the swans, was my first sizeable flock of wigeon of the season – a party of about 200. But now, the pool was calm and blue, and the sun lit up not only the birds but also the golden-buff twigs of the row of willows forming the backcloth beyond. I was just enjoying this pleasant scene when it became transformed into an even more idyllic and memorable one. Just as a party of four Canada geese skimmed the pool, honking as they passed, the wigeon replied with a chorus of their musical whistles, some of the whoopers raised their heads and emited a few bugle call notes, and at that precise moment the whole scene was framed within a perfect rainbow. This is now the 14th year in which whoopers have spent at least part of each winter in this specific area, although it is well south of their normal wintering range.

A COUNTRY DIARY 1981

Oxfordshire: Recently I received an inquiry from a reader in the south of this county concerning a bird, seen feeding on plough-land near her house, which was pheasant-like in all respects except that it had snow-white plumage. The query was whether this was an albino pheasant or an escaped bird from some wildlife centre. I must confess that at first I was somewhat surprised that my correspondent (whom I knew to be observant in such matters) had never encountered an albino cock pheasant before, for I regularly see such specimens, and have been familiar with them since childhood. But my experience is heavily biased by the fact that my haunts are still intensive pheasant-reserves, and the chances of mutants appearing amongst the thousands reared annually, are naturally greater than in smaller and more truly wild populations. Since such white birds are often deliberately spared in the annual slaughter, and may survive for many years, there is a good chance that their genetic peculiarities may be transmitted to their offspring. In the old days our local woodland was stocked with the original black-necked species which the Romans knew, but some neighbouring estates favoured the ring-necked variety from much further east than Colchis. The typical cocks of either race seemed to fit into the late autumn or winter scene just as acceptably as if they were natives, but now I find it difficult to accept them as a pure species, for the modern tendency seems to favour mutant strains, and a high proportion of our local stock consists of cocks of any colour from black to pale buff, and hens from a creamish tint to a reddish, black-tipped plumage which is quite grouse-like. But the general effect is of a mongrelish mixture, which may eventually be as far removed from the original species as are the motley hordes of London or feral pigeons from their rock-dove ancestors.

A COUNTRY DIARY 1982

Oxfordshire: In the hedges in my immediate vicinity considerable patches of elm – suckers – still survive, and recently, in a plantation of mainly young beech in our local forest, I was gratified to find that during current clearing of the undergrowth, apparently healthy elm saplings which had not been planted had been left unscathed. But so far I have not come across a single mature elm which escaped the ravages of the disease which has drastically altered our landscape during the last decade. But a few miles away, just over the Gloucester border, a correspondent informs me that recently he was delighted to find two splendid specimens of elm, about sixty feet high, still flourishing. He sent me a leaf, which, tentatively I have identified as that of the Huntington elm, a chance hybrid which originated as a nursery seedling over two centuries ago, and which thereafter was planted extensively for its ornamental value. Since, according to Alan Mitchell's league table of outstanding specimens, a Gloucestershire tree is (or was?) the finest known example of this form, it seems likely that these survivors, growing in isolation from any other elms in a Cotswold village, are of the same ancestry. The Huntington seedling came from a Dutch elm, the so-called *Ulmus hollandica*, which itself is considered to be a hybrid between two other species. But, in view of the apparent immunity of these two survivors, it is interesting to note that, just over forty years ago, Dutch arboriculturists raised what were then hailed as immune varieties from this same strain, but, alas, even these proved susceptible to the more virulent form of Dutch elm disease which struck some thirty years later. An ominous aside in my correspondent's letter is, 'I did just notice a very small branch dead at the very top of one tree.'

A COUNTRY DIARY 1983

Isles of Scilly: Like Fair Isle at the other extreme of the British Isles, these islands have become famous for vagrant exotic birds, from both far to the west and far to the east, which make landfalls when carried off-course during the spring and autumn migratory periods. But in this lovely south-westerly location the expectation is for North American involuntary visitors carried westward by gales during the 'fall migration' down the Atlantic seaboard of North America, and this October proved exceptionally productive. American species recorded were bobolink, Baltimore oriole, red-eyed vireo, red-breasted grosbeak, parula warbler, blackpoll warbler, Swainson's and grey-checked thrushes, buff-breasted, spotted and white-rumped sandpipers, sora rail, an upland plover, and a cliff swallow. The latter appears to be the first-recorded occurrence of this bird in Europe, and if, as it did during its few days' stay, it keeps company with the swallows and house-martins which were still abundant at the end of October, it may end up wintering in South Africa. Of course, on arrival we received the usual commiserations from other birders – 'you should have been here yesterday.' For many of the rarities had vanished, but I did manage to get good views of blackpoll warbler and upland plover on the islands, and a spotted sandpiper on the return journey near Penzance. But during my stay in the last week of October anticyclonic weather, with winds from the east and north-east, brought in the usual quota of strays from Eurasia, amongst which I saw Pallas's and yellow-browed warblers, a red-breasted flycatcher, and a little bunting, with innumerable goldcrests and firecrests.

A COUNTRY DIARY 1984/85

Oxfordshire: Throughout the hard spell, foraging among the hay and straw put out for the cattle, a flock of yellowhammers has frequented a field just across the lane from my garden. The recapture of ringed birds – two of them now at least five years old – indicates that they come to the same site winter after winter. But recently amongst them appeared a mainly pure white specimen, which at first, viewed from a distance without the aid of binoculars, I assumed must be a cock snow bunting. Subsequent examinations through binoculars at closer range revealed that it was too white, especially on the head, for a snow bunting in winter plumage. In view of the company it keeps, the likeliest explanation is that it is an albinistic yellowhammer. When a partial thaw began, the same field was immediately dotted with widely scattered redwings, and on spotting a white speck moving among the more distant birds, I immediately jumped to the conclusion that it was my mystery bird, but it proved to be yet another partial albino – this time a redwing. It had a white crown, a nearly complete broad white collar, white shoulder-patches, and pure white underparts apart from a few speckles on the throat and upper breast. In contrast with the white underparts, the normally brownish-red flush on the flanks (from which this species is misnamed) looked truly red. A puzzling aspect of these redwings, obviously finding food on a field with merely a film of water on hard frozen turf, is the nature of the morsels being obtained. I can only guess that minute snails, lying dormant in the remnants of the close-grazed tussocks, were being found.

A COUNTRY DIARY 1985

Oxfordshire: The chains of the large berries of black bryony are now conspicuous in the hedges among the frost-blackened foliage. Despite their attractive presence. the blackbirds and fieldfares feasting on the surrounding abundance of hips and haws appear not to be interested in these bright and succulent fruits. Yet, eventually they must fulfil their function and be eaten by birds, for seedlings appear in my garden. I have counted the berries in several chains and kept a periodic check to see if any disappear. In most years they remain untouched and wither rather than fall. Since it is in this state that they begin to disappear, I believe they form a last resort for hungry birds later in the winter after the hips and haws have been cleared. I have some (literally) first-hand evidence for this:

in midwinter a few years ago when the main hedgerow berries had been used up, I caught a wintering blackcap which obligingly left a tell-tale deposit in my hand, the seeds in which proved to be those of black bryony. Our other bryony, the white, although totally unrelated to its black namesake, seems also to be rarely eaten in its fresh state, although I have seen both garden warblers and lesser whitethroats taking the occasional berry. I suspect that its smaller and pinker berries, which also persist in a withered state, are also a reserve diet for birds.

A COUNTRY DIARY 1986

Oxfordshire: The dabchick or little grebe tends in winter to frequent waters where it does not breed. Some weeks ago there were seven on the reservoir I frequently visit, and last year I saw a party of 15 on a coastal freshwater pool in East Anglia. One assumes – or used to assume – that these birds were merely natives from nearby breeding sites, since it seemed unlikely that this species – rarely seen in flight except just skimming the water during mating squabbles – could be capable of undertaking long-distance migrations. The only personal evidence of aerial cross-country movement occurred some years ago when, on a foggy October night, one collided with overhead wires as I drove along a road far from water; after a few days in care, it was returned to a nearby pool. It had long been suspected that some of these winter birds are winter visitors from the Continent, but until recently the only supporting evidence was of a single example: the recovery in England some years ago of a Danish-ringed bird. But in the British Trust for Ornithology's 1985 report on ringing is proof that this bird is capable of much longer migratory journeys. One ringed as a youngster in Latvia in 1983 was shot in Lancashire last January, about 1,025 miles west-south-west of its home waters. The killing was not deliberate; a somewhat trigger-happy hunter had fired at bubbles which he assumed were coming from a mink just below the surface.

A COUNTRY DIARY 1987/88

Oxfordshire: My recent reference to my bird-ringing activities has brought a letter of protest from a reader who considers that the trapping and handling of wild birds should cease. She suggests that my fleeting visitors, if not interfered with, would stay; and so, one must assume, by the end of winter I would have about 500 tits and greenfinches swarming around my peanut-bags. I thought I had made it clear that birds once trapped and ringed did return for more, and that the intervals between such visits pointed to a nomadic winter existence. My critic also asks: 'What bird would want to return the next day if it been caught and handled and ringed ?' I could provide a long list of species in answer to this, but the current example will suffice: I have just recaught two coal-tits, one for the thirteenth time and the other the eighth, since I ringed them earlier this winter; and both, thanks to the free peanuts available, are in prime condition. As to the ring being a hindrance to its wearer: the fact that some large birds – such as shearwaters, gannets, terns, curlew, and eider – have survived in the ringed state for between to 25 and 30 years, and smaller ringed birds – such as chaffinch, blackbird, and blue tit – for up to 11 years, does not support this fear. Once, in late July, I caught and ringed a willow warbler, an adult, which must have already made three long-distance trips across the equator. The following year I recaught it at precisely the same spot in my orchard, and again in the third year. Since I did not come across it in the fourth year, I assumed that it had met its end, but in the fifth year it turned up again; the tiny ring on this equally tiny bird had certainly been of little hindrance on tens of thousands of miles of migratory journeys.

A COUNTRY DIARY 1988

Oxfordshire: Hereabouts buckthorn is one of the less plentiful of the berried plants in old hedgerows and in the forest itself. But in the bottom below my house there is the finest specimen I have ever seen; not the usual mere bush, but a tree some 20 feet high with five trunks varying from nine to six inches in diameter. A few weeks ago every twig was clustered with glossy black berries, and at the end of November I was surprised that only the odd blackbird showed any interest in them, for in most years the tree is stripped in September. On December 1 a flock of fieldfares descended on the valley, where I had noted the still intact crop the previous day, and on the 2nd the tree had been completely stripped. Since only flock-feeding birds could be responsible for such rapid clearance, it is pretty certain that the 'felts' (as they are known locally) reaped the harvest. An odd fact is, that although tens of thousands of seeds from this tree must be scattered annually in the droppings of fieldfares, blackbirds and redwings, I have yet to find a seedling in my garden, where to date my score for bird-introduced berried plants is 18 – 13 natives and five from other folks' gardens, these being two species of cotoneaster and one each of leycesteria, hypericum and mahonia. Fieldfares and redwings do not visit the garden until driven by food scarcity in hard weather, by which time the buckthorn will not be available, but the main planter of these 'volunteers' (the local gardeners' term for adventitious species), the black-bird, should by now have presented me with a buckthorn seedling.

A COUNTRY DIARY 1989

Oxfordshire: When, during the October gales, the ground beneath my Sturmer Pippin was strewn with windfalls, I attempted to harvest the remnant, but found that they were still firmly affixed to their spurs, and that those which had fallen had been wrenched off, spurs and all. This fine old variety, raised in Suffolk about 150 years ago, owes its aromatic flavour to another good old apple, Ribston Pippin, which was one of its parents. But, as a commercially viable variety in our climate, it has two drawbacks, firstly its lateness in ripening, and, secondly, in normal British weather, a dull russety-greenish colour which does not suggest the hidden flavour. But, thanks to the sunny summer, many of the topmost speci-mens on my tree are as flushed with orange and pink as the imported stock from Australia. Although it is assumed that birds have not a highly developed sense of taste, both tits and blackbirds, despite any flamboyant colouration to attract them, recognise Sturmers as worthy of attention, and those out of reach, when harder weather prevails, will, as in former winters, attract both fieldfares and winter-visiting blackcaps. In his comprehensive *Apples Of England*, Dr Taylor states that 'in England this variety only reaches full maturity in years of hot summers,' and goes on to say that 'indeed, November/December-picked Sturmers are the best,' and, with a basket-full of fine specimens picked for the first time ever in the latter month, I agree. A further bonus, as I now live alone and do my own catering, is that Sturmer is an excellent cooker.

A COUNTRY DIARY 1990

Oxfordshire: Having cleared the foot-deep cover of snow from the approaches to my house, and finding that the high-stepping gait needed for my usual walk in the fields was too exhausting, I settled down indoors to write Christmas cards. The recurrent theme of 'Happy Christmas' turned my thoughts to a memorable occasion long ago, when the wish became fulfilled in a spectacular manner. It was during World War One, and all the family but one – Dad, Mum, four girls and three boys – were about to sit down for a gloomy Christmas dinner – gloomy because the missing member of the clan, my eldest brother, was at sea, and his ship, the *Cameronia*, was long overdue, and feared to be yet another U-boat victim. Then in walked Ben, his ship having finally docked at Leith after a circuitous North Atlantic route. But, as so often happens, there was an anti-climax to the happy excitement – delving in his bag, my brother produced what at first appeared to be a bottle of whisky, and Dad's eyes lit up. But then came the apology, 'I'm sorry, dad, I did mean to bring you a bottle of Scotch, but I travelled down with a party of the Seaforths, and I'm afraid there's only a dram or two left.' May I wish all my readers, and particularly those who have written to me, an equally happy Christmas and New Year.

A COUNTRY DIARY 1991

Oxfordshire: Although the odd dandelion, dead-nettle, groundsel and other garden weeds may be found still blooming in winter, it seems that we have few native plants which are habitual winter-bloomers – locally I can only think of stinking hellebore in this category. Winter aconites and crocuses, although widely naturalised, are foreigners, whilst there is some doubt as to whether the snowdrop is indigenous. What has turned my thoughts to this topic is the scent from the wintersweet (*Chimonanthus*), now in bloom just beneath the window, and the mass of equally fragrant pink flowers on the large bush (almost a tree) of *Viburnum bodnantense* which adorns the background of a few yards behind. In our ancient churchyard a fine specimen of the winter-flowering plum (*Prunus subhirtella*) has excelled itself in its profusion of blossoms, whilst in front of the window where I write the bright yellow of winter jasmine sprawls invasively over the miniature terrace. Since all of these are exotic species, and mainly from cold regions of Asia and North America, two questions arise: why do we not have any winter-flowering native shrubs, and what advantage can such precocity bring? The scent of two of the subjects mentioned indicates that insect pollination is indicated – but what insects are likely to be available in Himalayan, Chinese or North American winters? The only likely pollinators of my viburnum are house sparrows and tits, which come daily to peck at the blooms. The Glastonbury Thorn traditionally bears both blossoms and leaves on Christmas Day. The earliest reference to this, when three such precocious specimens grew on the Tor, was in the early 16th century, but the myth concerning the miraculous sprouting of the staff of Joseph of Arimathaea first appeared in print about 200 years later. The truth seems to be that our native hawthorn may produce the occasional aberrant specimen of the Glastonbury type, for some years ago my late brother, Eric, found one, in full leaf and bloom, in midwinter in Thetford Chase, Norfolk.

A COUNTRY DIARY 1992

Oxfordshire: Amongst the spate of encouraging letters received from readers is one which, in effect, says 'never mind that you are no longer able to ramble around in search of topical matter – keep reminiscing about the good old days, for the benefit of us older readers.' Therefore, triggered off by the sight of bracken turning colour, I engaged in a train of thought. I remembered that, at this season, bracken was gathered as a nightly covering for the cold frames containing a wide variety of scented violets – blue, purple, mauve, pink and white, some single, some double, but all highly scented to provide Her Ladyship at the big house with a continuous winter supply. But what 'the men' (the garden labourers) gathered was then not known as bracken, as it was in our Scots household, but the southern 'fern', pronounced 'fee-urn'. Then my thoughts turned to the horses which carted the bracken from the heath, an area of Wychwood where, on high ground, a layer of acid sand capped the prevalent limestone subsoil, supporting a flora of heather (ling), gorse and bracken. A further mental diversion here evoked a memory of a scaring incident when, as a youngster brushing through the head-high bracken late one summer evening, I realised that a large, hawk-like bird was circling around my head. I was later assured that it was only a harmless 'Buzzing-'awk', the local name for a nightjar. I have since concluded that it was feasting on the moths disturbed by my passage. As to horses, the three which I remembered were Captain, Merryman and Short – the latter pronounced 'Shart', whilst the hard C of captain and the G of gate was followed by the intrusive consonantal Y, so that Cyaptain was pulling the cyart through Bicester Gyet. The latter name has no connection with the town suggested, but was a substitute for the unfamiliar Latin 'Vista'.

A COUNTRY DIARY 1993

Oxfordshire: In my boyhood the staple treatment for winter coughs was blackcurrant tea – made simply by pouring boiling water onto a couple of spoonfuls of blackcurrant jam, plus a spoonful of honey when available. Now, unexpectedly, I have come across another use for preserved blackcurrants, albeit rather therapeutic than medicinal. Somehow, a few weeks ago, I strained my shoulder muscles possibly by reaching too high when pruning the weeping buddleias over my entrance gates. Apart from massage and manipulation from a chiropractor and an osteopath, cold treatment was recommended by both consultants, and each enquired as to whether I had a packet of peas in the deep freeze which could be used as a cold compress. Mine have already been used, and all I had left were bags of loganberries, runner beans and black-currants. I chose the latter as being most malleable and in fact I have a bagful wedged in place as I write this. So far the treatment has acted as a soothing measure rather than as a cure.

A niece who is a *Guardian* reader has written me concerning the activities of a magpie visible from her window. Not only does it dunk dry bread in water before eating it but it also digs a hole in the lawn to bury surplus items and regularly finishes off each storing operation by searching around to find a leaf which it places over the burial site. The light falls of snow seem to have little effect on birds' feeding requirements; although my garden is strewn with windfall apples (since I am unable to pick those from the taller trees), only a few tits and the occasional blackbird, but none of the expected fieldfares or redwings, has taken advantage of the easy food on offer. But the chief variety concerned, Sturmer Pippin, will last till the really hard weather arrives, as I feel it will eventually.

Many people turned out to help plant the copse in Bill's memory in November 1995.

14

AND NOW ... ?

========

Bill was President of the Charlbury Society for many years and following his death, the Society met to consider a proposal for a local memorial to him. The Town Council offered to release half an acre on an island known as the Mill Field. The plan was to have it planted with native trees and shrubs, to attract the wildlife Bill loved. Several volunteers began work in November and December 1995 and two hundred and fifty trees and shrubs were planted and a seat installed. The density of planting was based on expert advice and thinning in the future is to be carried out as specimens mature. Some trees, like willows, hazels and alders, will be coppiced as shrubs and not encouraged to grow as full trees. Native black poplars, rare and particular favourites of Bill's, were planted in separate positions and not in the copse, since they will in time make large trees. It is hoped many people over the coming years will enjoy the interest, peace and tranquillity this island has to offer. In April 1996 a pair of swans became early and most welcome neighbours for the copse, when they nested a few feet away on the river.

Hilda Pipe, then Chairman of the Charlbury Society, chaired the committee which was set up to oversee the project, so she seemed the best person to supply an account of its activities:

The Charlbury Council gave a grant of £100 as well as the site on the Mill Field. It was accepted that, after several years covering the initial planting and conservation, the copse would finally become the responsibility of the Council. The appeal was launched in 1995, locally and nationally through the *Guardian*. In all £3680 was collected and so many of the letters that came with the donations paid moving tributes to Bill for the new insights into natural history that he had given people all over the country. The planting of the copse took place on a Saturday in November 1995 when a heart-warming collection of local adults and children turned out to help the Committee. The area was then fenced so as to avoid damage by motor-cyclists, picnickers and others, but it was planned that the fencing would be removed when the copse was fully established. A temporary notice-board was made and lettered by Selwyn and Moira Wyatt – this, too, to be removed and replaced by a more elaborate and informative one in a few years' time. A final touch was the installation of a teak seat with an inscribed tribute to Bill, sited beyond the further edge of the copse, where visitors and walkers can sit and enjoy the view. The Campbell Copse was officially opened by Jeannette Page of *The Guardian* on May 18th 1996, with speeches by Chris Mead of the British Trust for Ornithology, for whom Bill had done so much ringing work, and broadcaster Ken Jackson, who had done so much recording with Bill. It was a cold, wet day, but it was a tribute to Bill that over 100 people attended the ceremony, some of them local residents whom he had taught.

A photographic record of the making and opening of the copse was made by Jo Dunn, and this is now in the Charlbury Museum. The copse has been cared for from 1995 to 1999 by Peter Mond, and since 1999 by Christopher Betts. It is hoped that it will become a permanent memorial to a great naturalist.

Those invited to that opening saw that, as planned, it was planted with the trees and shrubs especially liked by Bill and is a lasting and living memorial to him, from those who remember all he gave to the natural world and to them.

There were many other tributes to Bill at that time, both written and spoken. Fortunately some of the written ones can be remembered here.

In the *Oxford Times* magazine, *Limited Edition*, there was an article by Elizabeth Seager under the heading, 'Harbinger of the Sun'. It was an appreciation of both Bill and the celandine and suggested that the double celandine is a living memory to this great Oxfordshire naturalist.

> Famous for his weekly nature columns in *The Guardian*, and *Oxford Mail*, and for local broadcasts, he was best known as an ornithologist, but was also an outstanding botanist and keen gardener.
>
> His Charlbury garden was full of interest, and he enjoyed showing off his February flowers – lime-yellow powder-puffs of *Cornus mas*, fragrant winter viburnum, slender lilac crocuses and rare yellow wild violets. He shared his treasures too, generously digging a root of January-flowering hellebore for me, as well as his double celandine.

Elizabeth Seager reminded us that Wordsworth loved the lesser celandine. However he cannot have known the double, which arrived on the scene in later years, but surely it would have been enjoyed in similar vein.

> See its varnish'd golden flowers
> Peeping through the chilling showers...
> Telling tales about the sun,
> When we've little warmth, or none...

The double celandine has a tight cluster of green petals at the centre of its double, glossy golden flowers. It shows its gold amongst bright green leaves, early in the year, just when we need reminding of more cheerful days to come and sums Bill's character up very well.

Hilda Pipe told us that when the appeal for contributions towards the Campbell Copse was made in the *Guardian*, money and letters came to the Charlbury Society from all over the UK. Many of the contributors said that although they had never met Bill, they felt as if they had lost a dear friend. Those who made contact with him always received a most generous response.

Miss Moira Russell wrote from Belfast: 'A few years ago I wrote to him after one of his articles mentioned living in Northern Ireland and got such a friendly chatty letter in return. Wasn't he marvellous in the way he kept going on to the very end, despite his disabilities?'

Miss Janet Campbell in Scotland: 'No more, alas, do I think to myself, "It's Wednesday – it must be W.D. Campbell." God bless his spirit.'

Charles Griffiths, Ruscombe, Berks: 'I trust the copse will be planted with such varieties that WDC could have chosen to cover his very wide interests.'

Gerald Small, Tring: 'His writings have given me much pleasure over the years and his philosophy I have found inspirational.'

Dr. Martin Skinner of the University of Warwick: 'While not being a regular *Guardian* reader, I used to make a point of buying it on Wednesdays just for W.D. Campbell's "Country Diary", and have done so since the mid 1970s. I liked it in the first place because birds are one of my great interests, but then I came to love the sorts of natural observations he made and above all those wonderful perspectives of time such as, "I went out with one of my old pupils who has long since retired..." or, "I was walking in a wood which I last visited in 1934..." etc.'

And finally from his *Guardian* fan, Richard Leighton, from Ilford:

'Regrettably ornithologists and nature lovers such as he are of a bygone era – the like of which we shall not see again.'

One of my most enduring memories of Bill involves an insect which is rapidly disappearing from the British countryside – the glow-worm. Of course it isn't a worm at all, but rather a rare beetle. I told Bill that when I was a child living in the Lake District, the grass outside our house during part of the summer and as soon as the light faded, used to be dotted with bright greenish little lights. I said how much I missed this childhood memory. One summer evening during the twilight hour, we heard Bill's voice and on looking out of a window of our home in the Cotswolds, saw him standing on the garden path holding aloft a glass container from which shone a soft green light. By finding, and temporarily 'borrowing', one of the very few Charlbury glow-worms, he had brought me pleasurable memories from my childhood, especially significant as he'd found it in one of his own childhood haunts, where they'd been abundant nearly eighty years before.

Ken and I both feel that we were immensely lucky to have known Bill so well and to have lived close to him, especially in his latter years. During the time of his failing health he had many visitors to cheer him – and be cheered by him – among them especially Peter and Phyllis Mond, who, with others, did much to repay him for all the pleasures he and his writings and broadcasts had given us.

Bill thought a great deal of Thomas Hardy and since he came in at the beginning of Bill's life, when the poet admired a very small 'WD' in his pram, it seems appropriate that this book should end with a quotation from one of Hardy's poems. Thomas Hardy's good friend William Barnes died, and at his funeral Hardy saw a sudden burst of sun throw its gleam on the coffin. When he returned home, he wrote a poem called *The Last Signal*, which ends:

> To take his last journey forth – he who in his prime
> Trudged so many a time from that gate athwart the land!
> Thus a farewell to me he signalled on his grave-way,
> As with a wave of his hand.

SOUNDS NATURAL

OVER 150 AUDIO CASSETTES, CDS, VIDEOS AND SLIDE SETS,
covering a wide range of Natural History, Wildlife, Conservation, Agriculture, Heritage, Drama and Poetry topics.

For the last twenty years of his life WD Campbell combined with Ken Jackson in many radio broadcasts for the BBC and he features in eight of the Sounds Natural audio productions, which are still available for you to be able to share in the magic and wisdom of his spoken words. These cassettes are listed below:

Westonbirt in Winter - Birds and Trees   SN 849
Ken Jackson joins Les Pearce, of the Forestry Commission, and W.D. Campbell for a February walk to identify some of the Arboretum's birds - and their songs and calls - and the trees which they're using.

Birds of a Broadleaved Forest   SN 850
W.D. Campbell and Ken Jackson take an early summer walk in a piece of ancient woodland to hear and talk about the birds there. Among the species singing and calling are: Garden Warbler, Willow Warbler, Blackcap, Lesser Whitethroat, Goldcrest, Robin, Song Thrush, Blackbird, Chaffinch and Wood Pigeon.

Nature Trail on the White Horse Hill   SN 854
A chance to join W.D. Campbell and Doug Jackson, who, together with Doug's sister Jo, took part in BBC Radio Oxford's Nature Trail programme from 1969 to 1980.   Their summer exploration of this lovely chalkland habitat includes a 'flashback' to an actual Nature Trail.

A Fungus Foray   SN 826
W.D. Campbell takes Ken Jackson on an Autumn walk through an Oxfordshire, mainly coniferous, wood in search of a variety of fungi, to explore their ecology, life cycle and edibility.

Wild Flowers and Country Cures   SN 839
W.D. Campbell takes Ken Jackson on a series of expeditions in the Oxfordshire countryside to find a selection of wild flowers and to reveal the facts - and fiction - of their medical virtues and vices.

The Nature of Christmas   SN 814
Ken Jackson talks to a variety of experts, including WD Campbell, about the natural history of Christmas animals and plants - Reindeer, Robin, Turkey, Goose, Camel, Ox, Donkey, Sheep, Norway Spruce, Mistletoe, Holly and Ivy.

An Autumn Walk in Wychwood   SN 877
Join WD Campbell as he walks with Ken Jackson along the footpath in Wychwood Forest, an area he knew for over 80 years. Share in its history, wildlife and dialect and some people 'WD' met - locals and visitors - over the years, and in two of his Wychwood poems.

The Nature of Poetry   TTT 833
A selection of country and wildlife poems, old and new, blended with natural sounds. Nature Notes by W.D. Campbell, plus two of his own poems, provide an interval at the end of side one and add background to some of the wildlife. £6.99

These cassettes cost £6.50 each, unless otherwise marked, plus 50p for postage.
They are available – as is the full Sounds Natural catalogue – from
Sounds Natural, Mid Boreland, Kirkcudbright, Galloway, DG6 4UY
Tel: 01557 339000   e-mail: kenaturalsounds@aol.com

Other books from the Wychwood Press

Wychwood and Cornbury
Charles Tyzack
£12.50 pbk   176pp   1 902279 04 2

Iron Age and Roman Wychwood: The Land of Satavacus and Bellicia
Tim Copeland
£12 pbk 144pp 1 902279 14 X

May Day to Mummers: Folklore and Traditional Customs in Oxfordshire
Christine Bloxham
£12.99 pbk 320pp 1 902279 11 5

My Three Hats
The autobiography of a schoolgirl at Milham Ford, a member of Stonesfield Silver Band, and a keen Oxford United supporter
Dorothy Calcutt
£8 pbk   112 pages   1 902279 25 8

The Salt of the Earth
Diary of a poor family in Woodstock, 1900
Dorothy Calcutt
£8 pbk   120pp   1 902279 06 9

Born in a Stable
The true story of John Ashton, illegitimate son of a Northumberland nobleman and an Oxfordshire village barmaid
Dorothy Calcutt
£7.50 pbk   1 902279 13 1   80pp

Discovering Wychwood
An illustrated history and guide
Charles Keighley (editor)
Includes about 100 photographs and line drawings, and two colour plates
£8.99 pbk   168pp   1 902279 09 3

Charming Charlbury, its Nine Hamlets and Chipping Norton
John Kibble
£10 pbk   224pp   1 902279 05 0

A History of Charlbury
Lois Hey
With a study of the town's geology by Professor Geoffrey Walton
£8.99 pbk   144 pp 1 902279 03 4

The Forest that Sailed Away
Poems by Elizabeth Birchall
Illustrations by Amanda Henriques
£7.99 pbk   64pp   1 902279 10 7

'Walk Humble, My Son'
Growing up in Ascott-under-Wychwood, 1918–1939
Eric R. Moss
Including My Personal Memories, *by Doris Warner*
£8 pbk   144pp   1 902279 07 7

Wychwood: The evolution of a wooded landscape
Beryl Schumer
£7.50 pbk 128pp   1 902279 02 6

Wychwood Forest and its Border Places
John Kibble
Foreword by Roy Townsend
£7.50 pbk 128pp   1 902279 00 X

Winchcombe: A history of the Cotswold borough
D. N. Donaldson
£14.95 pbk   272 pp   1 902279 12 3

Order post free from The Wychwood Press, Alder House, Market Street, Charlbury OX7 3PH. Credit card orders: 01689 870437.